I am not an academic, a legal scholar, or a man of letters—I am an Australian actor; I have been one since the early 1970s.

Recently I have become an activist for legal change.

You will understand why when you read my story.

Let's get right to the elephant in the room: Did I rape anybody? No.

Have I been raped? Yes, by a large young man who dragged me into the bushes when I was 13 years old.

I was brutally assaulted by a man when I was a child. I know what that feels like and that is why I fully support women and their continued empowerment to speak up through the #MeToo movement.

The human race needs to curtail sexual predators—full stop.

But, in the zeal to roll back centuries of entrenched male power, innocent men are getting swept up and mowed down. And false accusations are a danger to the real victims coming forward to share their stories.

I posted this quote in late October 2017 in support of the #MeToo movement:

'Verbal obscenities are horrendous.

If you find a woman attractive, say something flattering—not disgusting.

Stop the filth.'

A few weeks later at 4.30pm on Friday 17 November 2017 I received a phone call:

'You've been accused of raping someone forty-two years ago. It'll be on the front page of Saturday's papers nationally.'

ASSAULT BY MEDIA

The TRUE Story Behind the Headlines

JOHN JARRATT

adpublishing

Animal Dreaming Publishing
www.AnimalDreamingPublishing.com

ASSAULT BY MEDIA

The True Story Behind the Headlines

ANIMAL DREAMING PUBLISHING
PO Box 5203 East Lismore NSW 2480
AUSTRALIA
Phone +61 2 6622 6147
www.AnimalDreamingPublishing.com
Facebook: www.facebook.com/AnimalDreamingPublishing
Instagram: @animaldreamingpublishing

First published in 2019

Front cover photograph by Lint Gannon
Front cover design concept by Kerryn Williams
Final cover design by Richard Crookes
Back cover photograph of John and Rosa by Zadia Jarratt
Susan Jarratt, Consultant

ISBN 978-0-6486508-1-2

Designed by Animal Dreaming Publishing
Printed in Australia

CONTENTS

THE DOWNFALL

I'm writing this before my trial. This is day 371 since the nightmare began. I still have the devil's blackness tunic surrounding me and I can't get used to it. Looking at the footpath a year ago was easily the most horrendous moment of my life, a feeling no innocent human being should ever have to experience.

17 November 2017, 4.30pm. A café in the Adelaide City Markets

I'm enjoying a coffee with my daughter, Zadia. My iPhone rings; it's my agent, she sounds worried. I make my way out to the street, find a quiet spot and ask what the problem is. She tells me a woman has gone to the police claiming I raped her in October 1975. The woman then went to News Limited and told the same story. News Limited is going to put it on the front page of the Saturday papers and would like a comment on whether or not I raped this person.

I told my agent my comment was 'no', I then hung up as I'd lost the ability to speak.

I stood looking down at the concrete footpath for what felt like an eternity. I've been a public figure since 1975. In the 70s I made film after film, including break-out pictures like *Picnic at Hanging Rock*, *The Odd Angry Shot* and *We of the Never Never*. In 1980 I won the Best Actor Logie playing Ned Kelly in a four-part mini-series, *The Last Outlaw*.

I was in Adelaide in November for Supanova promoting the Wolf Creek franchise in which I play Mick Taylor, a role I'm known for internationally. Now, after forty-four years in the film business, all I could feel was being shrouded in blackness on a footpath, knowing I was about to be accused of rape.

I knew, immediately and instinctively, that that black cloud was going to be with me, like an evil outer skin, until I became exonerated.

My life was about to become hell on earth.

A hand was placed on my shoulder. 'Pappa, are you all right?' It was Zadia.

I turned to face her slowly, feeling helpless and bewildered. I couldn't figure out what to say. 'I... um... this is really bad... really bad. I've been accused of raping someone forty-two years ago.'

'What! What the fuck?'

I stumbled through what had just happened and as I told her she fell to pieces. She's very sensitive. Normally I bear hug her when she's upset, this time I just stood there looking at her like a crippled old man.

She recognised I was completely fucked and immediately got her shit together. She grabbed hold of me—the daughter became the mother. She spun me around, put her arm across my shoulders and took me to my hotel room.

There we both calmed down and tried to make sense of what had just taken place.

In October 1975 I was in Europe. My agent said the alleged rape allegedly happened in Sydney's eastern suburbs. (For some reason the name of the woman making these allegations was not made public.) I lived in Randwick in 1976, so the woman was a year out at this stage.

I said to Zadia it had to be The Female (what I'm calling her), with whom I had consensual sex in 1976. That was the first time I had ever cheated on my wife, Rosa, and I'm not proud of it.

(Rosa is my first wife and my fourth wife. We broke up in 1985 and got back together in 2011 after twenty-seven years apart. To find out how and why, read on.)

After this transgression, The Female stayed on at the house we all shared at the time and we both behaved as if nothing happened. She and Rosa had begun a friendship and she often joined us when we went out. It wasn't unusual for us to go to the Astra Hotel in Bondi on a Sunday where the two of them took over the pool table. They were excellent players. I wasn't. Never liked pubs that much but loved swimming, so I'd go to the beach and leave them playing pool.

In August 1976, I booked a Magnetic Island holiday for Rosa and me in late September. But I was offered a play, so I couldn't go, and it was decided that The Female would take my place. The two of them had a lovely holiday together. Strange way for a woman to behave who claimed I'd raped her, don't you think?

In November I was booked to do a film, *Summer City*, in which I'd cast two National Institute of Dramatic Art (NIDA) students, Mel Gibson and Steve Bisley. Rosa worked with the make-up department and I got The Female a job with the art department. She also played an extra in a bedroom scene with Steve Bisley.

The friendship with The Female continued until 1986, when I was playing the lead in a film called *Dark Age*, made in Cairns. The Female happened to be living there at the time and heard about the film in the local press, so she contacted the production office and left her number. I didn't hesitate to call her as I didn't have any reason not to. I invited her and her boyfriend to a barbecue on the following Sunday. After that she visited the set and befriended the make-up artist. They went shopping together and everything was tickety-boo. I was single by that time but I never went there; I wasn't inclined to and she had a boyfriend.

The film ended and the friendship just trickled away due to the tyranny of distance. No animosity at all. It was before mobiles and the internet and therefore hard to keep track of friends from afar.

The next time I heard about The Female was via that unforgettable call from my agent in 2017.

I then had to ring Rosa. She was so upset. I'm sure you can imagine how upset she was and, when you've done that, triple it. She then became angry—she's Sicilian. If The Female had witnessed her anger that day she would have dropped the sexual assault claim on the spot.

After she had calmed down, Rosa got into 'taking care of business' mode; she became my rock and she still is. Without her and my kids I'd be curled up in a cave somewhere far, far away.

Zadia and I picked up the phone and started notifying family and friends about what they were going to read the next day: 'Actor accused of rape' with a photo of me as Mick Taylor.

My daughter Ebony had the toughest task. She had to tell my granddaughter that Poppie J had been called a rapist, in case she was teased at school. The 10-year-old had looked at her mother and asked, 'What's a rapist?' Ebony had to explain. There are many reasons for writing this book, and having to tell my granddaughter is a very important one.

Another reason is this post by my 13-year-old son Riley on Saturday, 18 November 2017. We had to pull it down straight away. I read it and cried. But it's still absolutely relevant today.

As far as I'm concerned my son has more sense than the DPP.

I am not afraid to show this, I am not hurt or offended by anyone. No one in their right mind could make a joke about my dad being a rapist and to say he was a rapist from the 70's, which started about... 47 Years ago, that's right 47 years. Is one of the dumbest things I have heard in this modern day andtime. Who would ever believe a rape victim wouldn't come out about the story for 47-ish years? An exemplary headline would be 'Had sex! Does this mean I am a rape victim?' So if my dad or anyone else is worried this can affect me in any way at school or destroy my family reputation they are wrong. A headline is a headline, but a fake story is always a fake story.

Zadia and I went to the exhibition rooms at the Adelaide Showground to break the news to the Supanova team. The Zachariou family runs the show, headed up by Daniel. I explained my predicament and offered to fly home if he wanted me to. These people are like family to me, so much so that they made me their ambassador. Daniel said he knew me well and believed me.

'An innocent man pushes out his chest, holds his head up and carries on. Now go and sign photos for your fans,' he said.

It was about 9.30pm and Zadia and I were worn out with the whirlwind of dialogue and phone calls. I felt like I was drowning. We went to the bar and ordered a meal as it'd be the last time I could be in public for quite a while. As I was sitting there picking at some food, my big wonderful son Charlie, walked in. We had rung him at 5pm and he'd headed straight to Melbourne airport and flown over to Adelaide.

For the first time that day, I cried.

Saturday morning. The beginning of the toughest two days work in my life. I'd seen the front page of the papers: 'Actor accused of rape'. It was in every news bulletin on TV, radio and across the internet.

Charlie, Zadia and I went in to Supanova via a secret entrance. I was met by the effervescent Juanita, who was my minder for the day (love this crazy bitch), and my beautiful assistant Tony, who's a great friend and an ugly bastard, really.

We were taken to my signing table. A bunch of Supanova staff, led by Juanita, hovered around my table and kept the TV cameras and journos away. My daughter is quite tall and my son is a big dude, and they stood either side of me making it hard for cameras to get a good look. That nonsense went on for two days.

At these events I sign hundreds of photos. I try to give the fans a fun time and somehow I managed to keep that happening. Apart from the media, no one gave me a hard time. The people came to my table with their big smiles, but they had a look in their eyes that said 'you've been accused of rape'. It made things strange and uncomfortable. It was hard to get used to.

Months later that look remains in the eyes of the public—it makes me feel very sad.

We walked into Adelaide airport on Sunday evening. Two days of humiliation were finally over; what an endurance test! My kids were still protecting me, walking either side. We sat down for a coffee. I told them I needed to go to the toilet and Charlie offered to go with me; I said I'd be right. Mistake. It was a long walk there and back. I could feel people staring at me with *that* look in their eye. To the toilet, in the toilet and back from the toilet. I tried to look past them but it didn't work. I sat back down with the kids and I was frozen and couldn't talk. Zadia asked if I was all right and I fell to bits. Charlie put his arm around me, and I blubbed for him to take his arm away as people would stare.

After three days I had finally let go.

THE UPBRINGING

My dad had a saying, which he pumped into us regularly as part of his fathering:

'There are no medals for hitting women, son. Never hit a woman.'

'What if a woman hits me, Dad?'

'She's a woman. If you can't cop a slap from a woman, you're not a man.'

I've never hit, pushed or hurt a woman. Nor have I grabbed, groped or gutter talked to a woman. If I saw a man doing any of the above I'd front him and probably hit him. My parents taught me to respect women.

Dad was a coal miner. Five foot nine and 95 kilos of blood and muscle. He was a tough, bush bloke. Great rugby league forward and he could fight like a thrashing machine.

'Never start a fight, son, but make sure you finish it. If you're gonna get hit, hit first.'

Good advice.

I come from Wongawilli, a coal-mining village on the south coast of NSW. A kid's paradise. I still dream about Wonga, they are always beautiful dreams. If boys in the 1950s played up, your old man would give you a hiding; it was normal. Doesn't happen anymore, thank God, which proves society can change radically.

Girls got grounded and had to do housework. I have six kids, and I have never belted any of them.

I never swore in front of my mother, I was taught not to. I never answered back. I was taught not to. I did as I was told. I loved my mum, she hugged us, told us stories, played with us and sang like an angel. 'Over the Rainbow' was our lullaby. She used to say 'Why can't people just be nice to each other? It's easier.' She taught me to respect and protect women.

All his life when I asked 'How's it going', Dad?' he'd reply, 'I'm the luckiest man in the world. I'm married to the most beautiful woman in the world—inside and out!' And she was.

Dad was a binge drinker, as I was. A binge drinker doesn't drink regularly. They may not even have booze in the house. But every now and then at a party or some such event, they'll drink themselves into a stupor and often cause havoc. One night, when Dad was 39 and Mum 34, he came home rotten drunk. They had an argument in the lounge room. Mum got her Irish up and for the first time she slapped Dad, and for the first time he slapped her back. He gave up drinking on the spot and died sober forty years later.

He said to her he'd cut his arm off if he ever hit her again. 'Never hit a woman, son'.

I never have. I've been slapped a few times by women over the years, but I've never slapped back. I haven't had a drink or drug for thirty years.

If you mistreated girls in the 1960s you'd get punched. If you fancied a girl you would summon up enough courage to ask her out, usually to the pictures.

If she fancied you she might be up for a second date. And if that went well, you might get to kiss her on the third date. If you began going steady, she might allow you to get intimate, but very rarely did it go all the way. Around 17 or 18 years old, if you had a long-time girlfriend, there was a fair chance of your having sex.

The point is you had to earn it; you couldn't just take a girl unless she was easy and that was rare. Personally, I enjoy being loving when I make love. Sex should be a gentle, pleasurable experience. It could get hot, but never violent—where's the love in that!

In the mid-1980s I was with my old man and he needed to go to the bank in Sydney's west. I was in my mid-30s and Dad was early 60s. He was still fighting fit—we had mixed concrete in a wheelbarrow earlier that day. I decided to wait outside the bank. The next minute I hear his bullhorn baritone: 'John... John!'

I raced into the bank. Dad was standing fuming, staring down three punks.

I asked what was going on. He said, 'You take the two little blokes and I'll take the big piece of dog shit'. Straight away they ran from the bank.

Here's what happened: Dad had lined up behind an elderly couple. The three punks began talking dirty to the cashier who was quite a good-looking woman. 'I'd like to ram it up you sweetheart'; 'Bags go sloppy seconds'; 'I'd give her a length'.

My father growled, 'Shut ya filthy mouths or I'll shut 'em for ya!' One of the little punks said to his big mate, 'Punch the bald headed old arsehole in the head'. And that's when Dad called me.

That's where I come from, a mad Irish–Australian working class family. Sure, we've got plenty of faults, but we're decent and none of us is a sexually abusing predator. I did the show *Who do you think you are?* so I know who I am and who my family is.

In April 1971 I met the love of my life, Rosa, at her sister's wedding. She was 16 and I was 18. She came up to my family's table and said 'Why aren't you dancing?' I replied 'I'd like to dance with you'. She was the most exotic, beautiful creature I'd ever seen.

'Dance with me? Oh... OK'. She was my girlfriend from then until we became engaged in January 1973, and we married nine months later. I was faithful to her and remained so until August 1976.

One night in August, in a weak moment, I had consensual sex with a housemate. My wife was sleeping in an adjoining room. When I later joined Rosa in our bed I was full of remorse, riddled with guilt and absolutely disgusted with myself for cheating on her.

GOODBYE CAREER

Straight after Supanova I was about to begin a two-week publicity tour to sell Wolf Creek Series 2 for the streaming channel, Stan. Like the Supanova family, the Stan family means the world to me. They have stuck by me through this when others in the entertainment industry have abandoned me. Stan is beautifully led by its CEO, mighty Mike Sneesby, who has continually chanted 'I've got your back'.

Instead of doing publicity interviews on Monday morning, Charlie, Zadia and I sat in the Stan boardroom with lawyers. I've never been arrested, not even for being drunk and disorderly or driving under the influence in my youth. I didn't know how the law worked.

I do now, though, and I can also tell you how it doesn't work.

The lawyer informed me that historical 'she said, he said' cases like mine, with little or no evidence, usually were dropped. The downside was that it takes many months to happen. Again my guts turned, something that happens regularly these days.

As a result, I was virtually taken out of the Wolf Creek Series 2 publicity campaign, as we knew the media would only be talking about rape allegations. It was like selling a Wolverine movie without Hugh Jackman! Consequently, the series got off to a slow start but, fortunately, it's a great piece of television and the numbers picked up strongly through word of mouth.

I was also about to finish shooting a documentary for Stan comprising five, one-hour episodes about the Australian film industry from 1971 until present day. I'd already interviewed actors Mel Gibson, Bryan Brown, Helen Morse, Barry Humphries and Sam Neill, directors such as Bruce Beresford and Fred Schepisi, and several cinematographers and stuntmen. And I was in talks with distribution companies world-wide for copyright. (I'd negotiated many deals with big companies such as with Universal for *The Dressmaker.*)

But it all had to be cancelled—maybe forever. Two years wasted; I couldn't talk to actors like Cate Blanchett or Chris Hemsworth because of the rape allegation and I couldn't contact distributors for copyright. The Wolf Creek Series 3, my own feature *What About Sal?*... all the 2018 projects were gone.

The year 2019 was going to be my best year ever financially; Rosa and I were going to put a deposit on a home but my career is now on hold and I've been unemployed since August 2017. We're living at Rosa's mother's house and I'm on the age pension, all of which I give to my teenage sons for maintenance. Friends and family are helping us until this nightmare is over. At the age of 67 I'll come out of this massively in debt and unemployed. But hey, I'll be innocent!

THE STRUGGLE

Zadia returned to her house in Glebe, Charlie went back to Melbourne and I went home feeling lifeless. Rosa described me as a dead weight. I haven't smoked marijuana since 1985, but I felt stoned; I moved around the place like I was wading in treacle, just wanting to wake up from a nightmare. The lawyer said it was all going to take many months.

There is someone very close to me who's been raped and I know who the rapist is. He should be out of jail by now. I pray I'll never run into him as I'm unsure how I'd react. Ninety-nine per cent of rapists are males—I call them maggots. A woman of questionable values and motives has called me a rapist, resulting in my being associated with one of the most evil acts on the planet.

There are twenty-five million people in Australia and I estimate that twenty million have an idea as to who I am. They've seen me on their laptops, televisions, radios and in newspapers being headlined as a potential rapist, all asking 'do you think he did it?' The Goggle Box jury.

Five things kept me from lying on the floor in a foetal position wanting to disappear: one, my wife; two, my family; three, my friends; four, my late parents; and five, what and how I've been taught.

Only good people stay on top. The bad people are underneath, although some may delude themselves they are the ones up there. Good people can fall and go underneath—but not for long. The key is honesty. In AA it's rigorous honesty that I have aimed for. Too many powerful people in this world are rigorously dishonest and that's frightening.

My wife is my soul mate, my best friend and my rock. My six children from three marriages range from 15 to 41 years old. (I give each of my wives a house and two children!)

The love and support I have from my children and Rosa is immeasurable— they are an unbeatable team. My friends are pretty much the same, especially my Townsville mates. If the whole world disowned me, I'd turn around and they'd all be there, inches away. I don't know what you think of the afterlife, but I believe my mum and dad are with me at this time. My mum is the loveliest person I've ever met who always tried to do the right thing. Every morning of my life for many, many years, I'd get out of bed and tell myself the same thing.

I encourage my kids to do the same. I still try to do it, although, in weaker moments since the accusation, I sometimes wonder why I bother.

My dad wouldn't lie down if this nightmare happened to him, he'd fight like there was no tomorrow. When I'm feeling sorry for myself I suddenly hear Dad's thunderous voice: 'Man up!' Another thing he taught me was, if life becomes too much, go outside and yell at the sky: 'Is that the best you've got?'

Directly after the allegation became public I received over 300 texts and emails from friends and family. People I hadn't heard from in donkey's years. You know who your friends are when the shit hits the fan. I'm blessed.

The support for me has been phenomenal. It's held me up, kept me strong mentally, physically and spiritually. People believe in me and it's given me the incentive to write this book.

My friends in the entertainment business are right behind me and scared stiff they'll be next to be falsely accused. For all of the above reasons I hope to find a way to protect the innocent, especially those who are high-profile.

Replying to concerned friends and relatives took a lot of my time, and the weeks before Christmas were spent on research, trying to remember what happened forty-two years ago in 1976. I couldn't remember the street name in Randwick and had only vague memories of the layout of the house and the time of year the liaison took place. I was also trying to recall what, where and when events took place directly after that and for the next ten years, when I was still friends with the accuser. If you're as old as me it's hard to remember what you did specifically in 1976—I'm flat out remembering what I did last week! Rosa and I found a couple of photos from that time and that's it; however, they were significant photos.

All this was also really tough on Rosa who knew that I'd cheated on her with The Female.

The 1970s was peace, love, mung beans, sex, drugs and rock 'n' roll. I really enjoyed marijuana. Being in a party room with a bunch of stoned hippies listening to 'Dark Side of the Moon' having a 'love in' was very tempting to any 20-year-old, male or female.

And from 1971 to 1973 I went to NIDA in Sydney. I was a simple boy from North Queensland.

I was good-looking enough when I was young and was a fairly well-known movie actor from 1975 onwards. I didn't need to rape anybody to have sex. Rosa is a very beautiful woman inside and out, and I had no reason to stray. I look back at what an idiot I was to have strayed at all. As Paul Newman said: 'Why have hamburger when you can have steak at home?' Hear, hear!

In 1984 we had a truth session to put everything on the table. Over the years I'd had a few—not a lot—of indiscretions. I wasn't always sleeping around. I'd weakened a few times, usually when I was away for a long time on movie sets. But even a few is a few too many.

From 1984 on I learned the significance of being faithful. I tell my children, if they're in a relationship and want to sleep with someone else, have the decency to end their current relationship first.

TAKE A LOOK AT ME NOW

While I made the decision to end my second and third marriages, Rosa had made the decision to end the first one. I never got over her—she's been the love of my life since we met. I left my third wife in 2011. (By the way, none of my marriages ended because I was having affairs, including my first marriage to Rosa.)

In 2011 Rosa had a health problem and our two daughters, Zadia and Ebony, asked me to help with expenses. They went behind Rosa's back as they knew she wouldn't accept my help. She was very pissed off when she did find out but, at the same time, surprised and grateful. We began to see a bit of each other during her healing process and she came good in late October.

In October 2011 when we were both single I thought, bugger it, I'm going to try to woo her back. I was pretty obvious, although I thought I was being subtle. Zadia said to me over a lunch: 'Are you trying to crack on to my mother?'

When Rosa got wind of it she was absolutely astonished, describing us as chalk and cheese: 'Forget about it, it's never going to work,' she said. But I didn't, because I knew in my heart she still loved me. I persisted and I was let back into her life in January 2012. We married again at Palm Cove, Queensland on 12 March 2016 (my Mum's birthday).

In many ways we are different, but in others we are very similar. Anyway, whatever it is, it works.

Rosa is a very sensitive, emotional Italian. She is also sensible, strong and knows that what is happening to me is horrendous. She is nurturing, protective and has something stronger than muscles—she has integrity. If you mess with her husband and her family, you've crossed the line. The Female is so far across that line.

We are 'now and in the future' types, trying not to look back. Our first marriage ended thirty-three years ago. We both acknowledge we're very different people to who we were in our 20s and 30s, and have forgiven past indiscretions. Just before the nightmare began we were talking about how great things were looking. I had a contract with a considerable fee for Wolf Creek Series 3, an exciting documentary in the works, and was raising money for *What About Sal?* We were enjoying ourselves and having fun Googling real estate—then The Female decided to go to the police with her lies and try to ruin our lives.

Well, that's never going to happen.

To have a rape allegation is like having a broken arm. Everyone wants to know exactly what happened. It really hurts to tell the story once, let alone over and over again, but if a friend wants to know, I tell them.

Since November 2017 I've woken at around three in the morning. Sometimes the horror hits me straight away, or else I blink a couple of times and the unrelenting dread floods in.

And often the pain gets to Rosa— she's only human.

What will I do today? Nothing. Can't talk to anyone about projects or work. I've written two scripts to ease the boredom. I think they're good but I can't sell them until I'm found not guilty by law. I used to love exercising. DDP yoga one day, gym the next, but now I can't be bothered.

I used to eat great food but now I eat a lot of peanut butter on toast—I'm getting fat. I have managed to do a lot of walking and canoeing, which I do for hours in the bush or on the Lane Cove River. I use the time to concentrate on my plans for the future. I think about this book. And Donald Trump's come in handy. Never been into reality TV until he became the President of the Divided States of America. The man's more destructive than Godzilla. I didn't think the destroyer of planet America could be so amusing.

Endless days of trying to stay on top of this groundhog day of waiting for the allegation to be thrown out. My lawyer talked to the detective in charge of my case in March 2018. The detective said it could take weeks, maybe months, but not a year. It's the waiting that kills well-known people on media's death row.

MURPHY'S LAW

I had a great young lawyer; he already had the runs on the board and he seemed to be doing a good job. Mel Gibson, who's a mate of mine, has been very supportive. The paparazzi once tried to stitch him up but came off second best thanks to a lawyer called Chris Murphy. In March 2018 Mel advised me not to muck around, guilty or not—rape is serious. 'Your guy might be good, but Murphy's the best,' Mel told me. I took his advice.

The gregarious Chris Murphy rang me: 'What are you doing at 5.30am tomorrow?'

'Sleeping,' I said. He told me to be at a particular café in Darlinghurst.

I felt I was in a movie. It was still dark as I drove through the Cross and into Victoria Street. The neon lights in this faded hotspot were still on, but the seedy streets were empty. I parked the car and walked past a row of little cafés until I found Chris Murphy's 'office'. At 5.30 on a Friday morning it was already abuzz. A typical inner-city café with a small mezzanine level. Perched up there were three blokes, one I recognised as the famous Mr Murphy who introduced me to two lawyers who worked for him. Chris also invited a really good defamation lawyer, Bill Kalantzis who, coincidentally, was my lawyer when Channel 7 defamed me back in 2008. I won hands down.

Chris is in this café each morning as he feels he can have really effective 'one-on-one' meetings before dealing with all the distractions in his law office.

Thanks Mel: what an amazing bastard Chris Murphy is! He took me for a walk up the street and got me to tell him the full story. We returned and he told the other guys what was happening and how they were going to attack it. It became a strategy meeting. They knew each other really well and there was shorthand going on, much of which I didn't quite grasp. Chris gave them all their tasks and off they went. I stayed on with Chris who cross-examined me and made me really work hard to recollect things. He then sent me home to write a statement. I said I already had one from the last lawyer. He told me to file it and write a new one. He wanted it by Monday. He told me he'd never lost a case when he knew his client was innocent and he certainly wasn't going to let this one be the first.

The following week he read my statement and made some notes. He said I was a good writer and pointed out where I needed to be more precise and to remember more—think, think, think. I didn't feel that I could. 'Yes you can,' he said. He was right. Amazing what he's managed to extract from me and he hasn't stopped.

The following weekend he met Rosa, who felt he was very kind and considerate and at the same time, very smart. He was born and raised in Lakemba, cut from the same stone as Bryan Brown and Paul Keating: all 1960's working class, western suburbs boys. Rough diamonds—you wouldn't mess with any of them.

When my statement was completed, John Laycock, my lawyer who occasionally works with Chris Murphy, and I attended Maroubra Police Station. I read out my statement in the presence of Laycock, the detective in charge and another policeman. When I'd finished recording there was some small talk. The detective asked if I was going for defamation after the rape allegation was over. Laycock and I immediately locked eyes.

As soon as we hit the footpath outside we both spoke over each other. The detective had let the cat out of the bag when he was suggesting I sue for defamation. John felt it wouldn't be long before the cops dropped the case. He predicted July–August.

He was right—they threw it out through lack of evidence in August. The procedure from there was to send it to the Department of Public Prosecutions. My legal team believed they would bring the case to a close fairly quickly after that.

Below is my statement:

Statement of John Jarratt re police investigation of allegation

Name: John Jarratt

This statement made by me accurately sets out the evidence that I would be prepared, if necessary, to give in court as a witness. The statement is true to the best of my knowledge and belief and I make it knowing that if it is tendered in evidence I will be liable to prosecution if I have wilfully stated in it anything that I know to be false, or do not believe to be true.

I was born in Wongawilli, New South Wales on 5th August 1952.

I graduated from the National Institute of Dramatic Art and had my first film roles in *The Great Macarthy* and *Picnic at Hanging Rock* in 1974.

I met Rosa Miano in 1971 and we married in 1973.

In about April 1976 Rosa and I took a 6-month lease on a 3-bedroom rental property in Randwick. We rented our two spare bedrooms to help with the expense. One of the bedrooms was rented to [The Female*] the other bedroom chan-ged renters a few times.

In mid-1976, I had dinner with Chris Fraser the Director of *Summer City*. I had just won the leading role in the movie to be filmed starting in late 1976. It was a popular cast of Australian actors and included television star Abigail and radio's Ward Austin. It was a big opportunity forme.

After the dinner with the Director I arrived home at Randwick and my wife had already gone to bed. I went upstairs to where our bedroom was.

The three bedrooms at Randwick were upstairs. There were two bedrooms side by side and my bedroom, where my wife was sleeping, was separated by the bathroom in the middle from [The Female's] room.

When I got to the top of the stairs I first went to the bathroom to the toilet. When I came out of the bathroom I saw [The Female's] door was slightly ajar and she was loud whispering to get my attention. She invited me in to talk about the dinner I'd had. I talked about the film. One thing led to another, it gotintimate and we both willingly participated in consensual sex. While we were having sex [The Female] kept asking me to keep it quiet so we wouldn't wake my wife.

After that [The Female] and I carried on like nothing had happened. We never spoke about it again. [The Female] continued living there and was at all times friendly. Rosa and [The Female] were very good pool players and when winning they held the pool table against many challengers at the Bondi Astra when we went there most Friday nights.

Towards the end of our lease at Randwick in October of that year 1976, Rosa and I had booked a holiday flying to Magnetic Island. Unfortunately, because I was cast in a play with the Sydney Theatre Company, I could not go. I gave [The Female] my ticket to go with my wife and she took my place and flew to Magnetic Island with Rosa.

The third bedroom at the Randwick house in 1976 was rented for a period by a surfer a 'man mountain' we called

'Tree' I can't recall his real name. While he was there [The Female] had sexual encounters a number of times with Tree. [The Female] had no feelings towards him. She said she had slept with him a few times and just enjoyed the sex. It was obvious to us all that Tree fell madly in love with [The Female] and it became difficult in the house for all of us.

The housemate 'Tree' was being nasty and angry and horrible to [The Female] and wouldn't stop and it went on for days. He complained constantly in terms 'I have been used and thrown away!' He was so persistent and demonstrative about it that we told him he could not rent the room any longer and I asked him to leave.

Not long after Tree had left the house he came back to the place one night furiously inebriated and was out on the street yelling for [The Female] to come out. Then he started banging onthe door.

It was an emergency. I told Rosa to take [The Female] into the kitchen and lay low. I went out and confronted Tree. He was holding a large size bottle of beer, he was 6' 5" and about three stone heavier than me. He screamed at me he was going to knock the front door down. I told him he'd have to knock me down first. I was afraid I'd be glassed with the beer bottle. He stared at me for a while and stomped off.

I put myself at serious risk that night to prevent [The Female] from being harmed but I would always feel it my duty to stand in harm's way to stop a woman being violated or hurt by someone.

In November 1976 as the lease was due to expire Rosa and I left Randwick and arranged to live at Catherine Hill Bay for the following months while Summer City was being filmed. My wife was engaged to do the hairdressing and make-up work for the cast.

When [The Female] asked could she join Rosa and I and go with us to Catherine Hill Bay. I welcomed her to join us. There had never ever been any unfriendly issue with [The Female]. [The Female] wanted to be part of things. I got [The Female] on the crew of the film and she was given a small part where she was lying in a bed while actor Mel Gibson was talking through a window to actor Steve Bisley who was in the room with her.

We didn't see [The Female] much after the filming. In 1977 my wife Rosa was now pregnant and we moved to Coasters Retreat for a year, near Palm Beach Sydney before we built a house on Scotland Island where we lived for almost seven years.

At that same time [The Female's] new boyfriend had a job that took them around the country. It was the days of no mobiles or Internet. You lost track of people through the tyranny of distance so I don't remember seeing her much.

In 1978 I remember when [The Female] lived with another boyfriend on the NSW north coast. While I was driving to Brisbane I called in on [The Female] with Rosa and we showed her our infant Zadia. It was a normal meet up of friends.

In 1981, I was engaged in the movie *We of the Never Never* being filmed in the Northern Territory. My wife Rosa and daughter went to Cairns where she met up with [The Female] who showed her a screen printing business she had with her boyfriend at that time.

In 1984, Rosa and I were having marriage problems, it was about a number of problems that many young married couples go through. We decided to have a truth session and cleanse our lives of the past and start out fresh. I told Rosa the absolute truth that [The Female] had invited me into her room and we had willingly joined in having sex while she [Rosa] wasasleep.

In March1985, my marriage with Rosa ended. Things just weren't working out for either of us.

In March 1986 I had the lead role in *Dark Age* about a man eater giant crocodile. It was filming in Cairns. It was a big publicity affair. Quentin Tarantino later bought the original film. It was a major production with a big budget and a huge animatronic crocodile was built in thetown.

One day I was notified by the production office that they had been contacted by a woman who said she was a friend. I was given [The Female's] name and number and I rang her and invited her to catch up with me.

I had no issues with [The Female]. I had never done anything to her. I was always kind to her as a friend. There had never been any unpleasantness or arguments between us. I invited [The Female] to things. She came to a film company barbeque we were having and then she came on the set. [The Female] enjoyed herself mixing socially with the crew and cast. [The Female] became a regular visitor while I was there.

My relationship in that time in Cairns then was purely platonic I was between marriages at the time, but I didn't have those type of feelings for [The Female]. I liked her, apart from our mutual indiscretion; I had no reason not to.

I haven't seen [The Female] since the Cairns filming. We simply lost contact and the friendship faded. The next time she came into my life was on the front page of the *Daily Telegraph* with a photo of me from *Wolf Creek*. The headline read 'Wolf Creek Star in Rape Claim.'

My father raised me to respect women and that's how I am.

Dad used to say 'There's no badges for hitting women son.' I have never hit or hurt a woman physically, I've never belted my kids. I have never been aggressive or forceful towards a woman. It is unimaginable to me that I could ever have sex with a woman against her will.

If I'd run into [The Female] the day before the headline, I would have greeted her in the usual pleasant way. There was no reason not to of which I was ever aware. Now more than 40 years after our friendship was formed and continued I am confronted with this untruth.

This false allegation has been a sad and heartbreaking situation deeply affecting me and hurting my family. Having to explain this scandalous lie that has been published to my children and grandchildren has caused me grief. I repeat emphatically I did not have non-consensual sexual contact of any type with [The Female] and I would gladly undergo a lie detector test.

DATE:
SIGNED BY JOHN JARRATT
WITNESS:

**Name redacted for legal reasons.*

***

I have The Female's statement; I don't wish to have two pages of her words in my book. I will include five sentences from her describing the lead-up to the alleged rape to demonstrate how absolutely ludicrous this whole thing is.

Quote from her statement:

I got woken up by a person pulling the covers right off my bed. It was such a violent movement that the sheets and

> blankets were ripped clean off my bed and onto the floor. The next thing he did was to tear my undies clean off me. They were completely ripped off me in one movement and he tossed them to the side. Next John tore my t-shirt, he ripped it right in the middle with one big rip.

And that was just the beginning; she went on to describe the implausible rape. It makes me ill just thinking about it.

Now I'm a big butch bloke from the country. I can hold my hands up and I'm not a coward, however... if I was sound asleep and somebody woke me by pulling the sheets and blanket off my bed and ripping off my t-shirt and undies I'd be making loud noises. If the person then jumped on me and brutally raped me, you'd hear me yelling loud enough to wake the neighbours, let alone my wife sleeping in the next room. The Female claims she didn't make a sound.

My wife Rosa slept in the next bedroom and she didn't hear a thing. A man called Tree was asleep in the other bedroom and heard nothing. The Female remained my friend for another ten years.

WHAT? CHARGED?

On 25 August 2018, my phone rang. The name John Laycock came up. I was excited—the case had been dropped and my nightmare would be over. I was in a meeting in the Blue Mountains and I excused myself and took the call outside in the carpark.

'John, I've got some bad news—you've been charged.'

'You're kidding?'

'I'm not. Murphy's in shock, we all are.'

Once again I'm looking down at concrete, again my guts are turning. The devil's blackness tunic, worn since November 2017, began to smother and crush me like a python.

The DPP supposedly read the statement from The Female and charged me with rape on 25 August 2018.

I can only conclude that all that registered with the DPP was 'John Jarratt, accused rapist', and he or she got scared because the public knows of me. If that's not the case, it is a mystery to me who decided to charge me after reading the reports. On the other hand, I haven't studied law.

Already I could hear the Goggle Box jury: 'He's been charged, he must have done something!'

It's all going to get worse. My poor kids, my granddaughter, my Rosa. I just can't do all this. Then Dad turns up: 'Man up, John, man up!'

And I found myself yelling at the sky: 'Is that the best you've fuckin got?' I didn't care who heard me.

I had to go back into the meeting and pretend nothing had happened. Then I left and went around to my old friends, Nick and Joanne, who wanted help breaking out a wall (I'm an actor/builder).

Joanne Samuels played Mel Gibson's wife in *Mad Max* among many other things. I've known her since 1973; she's like a sister to me, and thank God I was going to see her that day.

I told her I'd been charged and was going to trial—then fell to pieces in her arms.

Late in the afternoon I drove from the mountains listening to the ABC radio news. I was the lead story. I arrived home to a distraught Rosa. She was beside herself that I'd been charged and nearly collapsed when I told her the trial would be at least a year away. I tried to comfort and assure her. As Mum always said: protect and respect.

Television crews had come to our house before I got there. First the bastards ambushed my shy 88-year-old Italian mother-in-law, who was overwhelmed by everything that had happened to me. Then they tried the same thing on Rosa, who handled them beautifully.

'Who are you and what are you doing here? This is my home.'

The female journo told her they were from Seven News: 'Your husband's been charged with rape.'

'Did I invite you here?' asked Rosa. 'No, you've no right being here and I'm asking you to leave.'

I ventured out on Saturday morning, thinking the coast was clear, when a paparazzo came running up the street. He was saying rape a lot while filming me. I said: 'Ridiculous and untrue, mate, I'm fine, because I'm innocent'.

My 24-year-old son William, a fantastic singer, turned up from Melbourne to be with me for a week. 'I'm here for you, Pop; where you go, I'll go.'

I'm blessed.

WRONG

I'm not a criminal, never have been, but, admittedly, in my youth, I did wrong things and justified them. I cheated on my wife but, hey, I was away on location for two months. I got rotten drunk and made an arse of myself but, hey, it was the first time in three months and I deserved a drink. I smoked dope all weekend and sat around like a zombie but, hey, that's cool.

In April 1985 my marriage to Rosa was over, for a number of reasons. It all started with my drunken self and a drunk woman in 1983. I cheated on Rosa, she found out and we went downhill from there. We both tried hard to bring it back together, but we didn't have the maturity to do it.

In the end she asked me to leave. I lost the love of my life for doing a number of wrong things.

I had to look at myself. I didn't drink much, but when I did, I drank to excess; I was a binge drinker. It caused me a lot of trouble, so I gave up drinking.

My dad once said to me: 'It's called dope, son, it's not called intelligent.'

He was right. I gave up all drugs. I gave up smoking when I was 22. I have tunnel vision—my way or the highway, I had to delete my ego and find compromises. Fight or flight, I ran away, and I had to learn to stay and face it. Many, many things needed sorting. My mother was a huge influence. She always tried to do her best and to do the right thing. That is now my daily mantra.

One of the greatest wrongs is to cheat on your partner. I haven't done that since I lost the love of my life in the 80s.

I've come up with the perfect diet, it's very simple: 'Don't eat the wrong food'.

You don't have to be a genius; everybody knows what the wrong food is. What I'm trying to say is, if we all tried not to do the wrong thing, the world would be amazing. It's wrong to rape, it's wrong to sexually assault, it's wrong to physically hurt people, especially women and children, it's wrong to murder—everybody knows this. It's wrong to hate, it's wrong to discriminate; that leads to riots and war.

It's wrong to steal and to lie. Lies can be so wrong that they're evil. The woman who accused me of rape told an evil lie—wrong.

Lying is a biggie. If you're honest, rigorously honest, then it's hard for you to do the wrong thing. The trick is to be honest with yourself. If you believe in a higher power, in God, then you know you can't lie and get away with it. Why put yourself through it? Tell the truth, relax and enjoy life.

Nobody's perfect; you're gonna fuck up, but don't beat yourself up. Nelson Mandela said he didn't have failures, he had successes and things he had to learn from. Learn from it and try not to do it again. It's called growth. It means you need to change, otherwise you could be a genius and an emotional infant at the same time.

It's scary to change for the better. We're all comfortable in the same old patterns, even if they're not good for you. My dad used to say he was born with a bad temper—not his fault just the way he's made, get used to it. You can't teach an old dog new tricks. Crap. I spoke to a wise old man thirty years ago. I told him: 'I'm like my dad, I lose my temper'.

He said: 'It's your temper, why would you want to lose it? Next time you feel you're losing your temper, walk away and don't come back until you've calmed right back down to fuckin angry.'

I haven't lost my temper since. You *can* change for the better.

Do it! We all deserve a good life.

On the other hand, life can throw you a whole lot of misery no matter how hard you try to be the best you can be. Look what they did to Jesus, Mandela and Martin Luther King. In Mandela's case, he still woke in his cell every day for twenty-seven years and stuck to what he thought was right and did the best he could under the circumstances. People like these have helped me get through being an accused rapist for a year and a half. A well-known friend of mine, who's also been through public hell, has been very supportive and very wise. He suggested that sometimes you go through public injustices because there's a lesson and a reason for it. Maybe I'm the person who can help bring balance and fairness to this travesty of justice I'm going through.

That is why I'm writing this book *Assault by Media* and I've made a documentary sporting the same title.

Staying on top of things and not assuming the foetal position is a daily task. At the time of writing this chapter there may be many months to go before the trial some time in 2019. A long, long time to be under what is virtually house arrest, staying away from twenty million stares: 'He's been charged—he must have done something wrong'.

The thing that's happening is wrong, terribly wrong, and my life's mission is to do things right. My family is covered in muddy media dirt. I'm not stopping until every grain of that mud is washed off, beginning with my granddaughter who's in her first year of high school.

I will change things for the better. I'll hope the people who've wronged me will one day be sorry for what they did to my family. Maybe they'll stop jumping at the excitement of a juicy headline and learn some humility. Hitting someone in the head with humility is much more progressive than hitting them with a right hook.

JUST GOT ANOTHER SIX MONTHS

It's been over a week since I last wrote. There's a reason for this. On 7 December 2018 I went to court to receive my trial date. We were hoping for March or April 2019, but unfortunately it's 1 July 2019. This took the wind out of my sails. Another seven months of hiding in my house.

After a few more rants to the sky, I'm ready to get back into it. I might not be employed as an actor at the moment, but that doesn't stop me writing this book, shooting my documentary, completing my programs on the film industry, and making my feature film, *What About Sal?*

The only hitch is, right now, I'm not being paid for any of my projects. They'll be ready to go when I'm out of court. I'm coming out of there not guilty, and I'll hit the ground running.

I'm writing this book to hopefully help my fellow humans. I live with a fellow human, who happens to be my love and my best mate. I'd love it if all my films were shot in my street so I didn't have to live in a hotel away from her. Don't get me wrong, we give each other space and we're proud individuals. Most men and women live together contentedly enough. Very few of us are violent thugs or perverts.

So let's keep this whole #MeToo movement in perspective. Just a reminder, members of this movement are the victims of male maggots. I've been raped by one and am a supporter of #MeToo.

I keep asking myself, 'Why me? Why on God's earth should I, of all people, be charged with rape?' I think the answer is that I have to do something to stop these tragedies and because I've been accused of rape I'm the best person to talk about all this.

That rape never happened. I've never belted women or children, never groped a woman nor used sexually abusive language to one. I try to be as Buddhist as possible—but you can't take the Irish out of me.

I think the #MeToo movement has swung too far and needs bringing back to the middle, especially for people well known to the general public. Apparently, the number one workplace for sexual abuse and misconduct is accountancy firms. If a male boss of one of these firms was using inappropriate language to a young female employee and at the Christmas party slapped her on the arse, the female should report him to the board of directors, human resources department, or whatever is appropriate. If it's severe enough, take it to the police. Don't bother taking it to the media, they won't even look at it—unless the guy is well known. If he is it'll be on the front page. Doesn't matter whether the guy's guilty or not. Why?

Freedom of speech? Nah! Money, ratings, sales distribution dollars. They'll stretch the story out for weeks; the well-known guy's life is ruined and he's in hell. Which is fine if he's guilty.

However it's an absolute abomination if the guy's innocent. There's nothing worse, believe me!

EVERY NIGHT

Monday, 17 December 2018. One year and one month, 396 days and nights since the nightmare began.

I can't get this out of my head. I dream about it every night. It wakes me up every night. I lie in bed looking into the dark. I've stopped having my phone next to me as I was checking the time every five minutes. This endless dream complicates everything and makes no sense of anything. Sometimes I can get back to sleep. Not very often. After half an hour of being awake I get up, go to my desk and look at the time. It might be 1am, often it's 3am and sometimes 4.30am, which it is this morning—I've slept in!

Rosa has always woken between 5 and 6am. I bring coffee, which we drink in bed.

She asks how I've slept, and whether I've had any dreams, but I don't want to talk about it.

But we do. Every second day we say to each other desperately: 'We've got to stop'. But we don't. Each day we think about it and the nightmares persist. Every twenty-four hours I Google my name... I have to be the first to know if there's some more shit about me in the media. You may be reading this book in 2020, Google me. I guarantee it will still be there.

I don't particularly want to watch TV, read or do anything. I just sit and stare, feeling like I've been put upon for no reason. The last time I went to court I was fronted by the cameras and journos who all seem to be squawking: 'rape, rape, rape, rape, rape'.

Every news outlet seemed to be covering it. I went to court to get permission to attend the district court on 7 December, a week away. Apparently I'll get my trial date for 2019. My trial date: it's 1 July 2019. We were hoping it would be a couple of months from now. It could have been much worse, it could have been twelve months away. Another year of this may have beaten me. I don't know if I'd have the strength. I'm already 66. There's much I want to do, spending years getting over all this mess isn't on the agenda. I'll cope with the seven month wait for 1 July.

Rosa is with me, as she always is, but in a way I feel so lost and lonely. I feel like I'm sitting on my lounge chair on a small barren island in the middle of a Siberian lake surrounded by ice and snow. If it wasn't for her I think I'd just want to go to a beach in North Queensland, live in a one-man tent and leave my family alone. I don't want them to have to continually hold me up. I'm living off the generosity of friends and family. I have no energy; I'm blank and my head's fuzzy.

I probably feel like this once a week. The rest of the time I'm up, I'm going to win and I'm going to do the best I can. This is when I don't write this book. The irony is I'm writing now so it's a cathartic thing, really.

Anyway that's enough of me feeling shitty. I'm going outside now to yell: 'Is that the best you've fuckin' got?' See, feeling better already!

I'm back. I chose a really faint star to yell at. One which was many light years away.

July 2019, my everyday nightmare stops.

FINANCES

The moral of this chapter—never get divorced.

In 2002 I was working on *McLeod's Daughters* in a supporting role. I earned reasonable money and I was just getting back on my feet from my second divorce in 1999. I'd managed to buy a run-down fibro cottage on Scotland Island in Sydney's northern beaches and rebuild it into a two-storey modern home. I had a 1-year-old son and one on the way.

My children from my second marriage, Charlie, 13, and William, 6, had recently moved with their mother to Mount Tamborine in Queensland. I wasn't close enough to them, so we sold the Scotland Island home and moved into a federation farm house on two acres at Murwillumbah, an hour away from Mount Tamborine, in April 2003.

I managed to buy the two small homes on a few acres which surrounded our new home. I went into debt, but I was empire building. Two years later, I made the dumbest move.

I was blindsided by an entrepreneur in Brisbane. He was very convincing. We formed a movie production company which initially went well. He convinced me to move to Brisbane in 2005. I got burned. I lost money and learned a lesson.

I moved the family to Brisbane. We bought a house on acres in southwest Brisbane.

In 2007 I turned 55 and was old enough to spend my super. I built a massive swimming pool and an extensive entertainment area which blew the lot—$150,000.

Then the financial crisis happened. We sold our Murwillumbah properties at a loss. I produced, wrote and acted in a movie called *Savages Crossing* and it tanked. More debt.

In 2008 we decided to move to the Sunshine Coast. We sold our Brisbane property for a little less than the price of the Sunshine Coast property. I continued to work, but we were just keeping our heads above water. The new house was a Queenslander, but it was small. I bought another three-bedroom Queenslander and transported it to the property. I joined it to the existing house, and spent about $200,000 totally renovating it.

In 2011 my marriage broke up. There was a property slump in southeast Queensland, especially on lifestyle properties like ours. I had doubled the size of that property but it took two years to sell and I ended up selling it for the same price I'd bought it for in 2008. Massive loss.

I gave my ex-wife and two sons everything. By 2013 I had Rosa back in my life. I owned a second-hand car and was in a whole lot of debt—personal debt, tax debt, credit cards, you name it.

By the end of 2012, I was supposed to be making *Wolf Creek 2*. We had a big budget and I was being paid a lot of money. This was going to save my arse. At Christmas 2012 I received a phone call from the producer. He had just moved to live in Adelaide for twelve months and filming was about to start. The major investor pulled out millions and the production immediately ceased. I became unemployed, broke and more in debt.

In late 2013–early 2014 we finally made *Wolf Creek 2*. The budget was halved and my fee drastically reduced. To counter that, I was given a big back end. Everyone agreed it would be very successful and I would make a lot of money out of the profits.

Didn't work out that way. It did well in Australian cinemas, but didn't make the budget back. The overseas distributor crashed the film into a wall and we received two million illegal downloads in six months. We lost millions. I made nothing from that film.

In 2016 I was about to crawl out of the massive debt hole. Stan backed a six-part Wolf Creek TV series. Series 1 halved my debts and in 2017 Series 2 would take care of the rest.

In September 2017, Rosa and I decided to start clean. What a good feeling it was. It took a massive chunk out of my *Wolf Creek 2* earnings but I wasn't worried as I'd already negotiated a contract for Series 3. It was going to be signed in July 2018: 2019 was about to become the most financially successful year of my life!

Until I got the dreaded phone call and the beginning of a year and a half in the wilderness.

It's now 23 December 2018. I've earnt zero dollars since August 2017. Wolf Creek Series 3 has been dropped. I'm maxed out on five credit cards, my tax bill is again way up as I've spent 2016/17 GST, and to keep Rosa and I going I've borrowed a considerable amount from a dear friend, which I must, of course, give back. I haven't been able to pay my teenage boys' maintenance, school fees or medicals for six months, and all my pension goes to them. I have the best lawyer in the business and he and his team are working for nothing.

They're not asking for anything but I can't work that way—one day I will pay them.

At the end of my trial, The Female will walk away guilty but because she's the alleged victim she not only receives anonymity, she gets free legal representation! She will be found guilty and it won't cost her a cent.

I will leave broke and unemployed, with a family severely victimised and publicly humiliated.

But the law will find me not guilty—hoo-bloody-ray.

CRASHING

Before November 2017 when this dreadful and bewildering allegation descended upon me, my prospects for 2018/19 were brilliant. I was the ambassador for both Asbestos Awareness and Supanova, which annually earned me quite a few grand, and I had a pay-or-play contract for Wolf Creek Series 3.

From these three gigs I would have earned around $500,000 —all were cancelled because of the allegation. I haven't worked since, nor have I received any offers in almost two years.

Without informing me, Screentime edited me out of its comedy show *Orange is the new Brown*. I only found out when I saw that I didn't appear in any of the promos.

(By the way, Screentime puts together the Wolf Creek Series—clearly loyalty isn't part of its mission statement!)

Below are several emails received from some very caring people:

Hi John,

Just some more notes on the fallout of this allegation.

As you know, I'm in LA to support the release of the new series—however that's now been cancelled indefinitely by the POP NETWORK, who releases the show in the US. Season 2, like Season 1, would have been available to 73.8 million households across America. That's how many homes POP is available in over here. A massive marketing campaign across the US was about to begin featuring yourself, the other main cast and me. As well as a press day for US media promoting the series—this has been cancelled also.

Production on Season 3 has been cancelled—or at least put on hold until the case is heard.

This means the 150+ people who work to make the series in Australia (producers, writers, actors, crew members, post-production teams), not including the hundreds of people who work for the marketing and distribution partners in the series around the world, now will not have those jobs.

It also means that the four feature films we already have written—that you are to star in and that would have employed approximately 150 cast and crew for each film (so 150 X 4 = 600 people) will now be on hold until this case is resolved. Because WOLF CREEK is a unique, independent Australian feature film franchise that is globally recognised, the demand for future series and movies is at an all time high. So financing and distribution—two things that are notoriously difficult to attain in our industry—were moving into place because of the high quality we continue to strive for and attain with each new film or series.

So adding series 3 and the 4 feature films already written and planned together, that's 750 jobs that will be lost because of this allegation. Not to mention the irreparable brand damage that's been done to one of Australia's most recognisable entertainment success stories. Not sure if you're aware but our little movie made the list of the top twenty-five Australian films of the 21st Century. Next to Crocodile Dundee and Mad Max, Mick Taylor and Wolf Creek have become Australian Icons.

https://www.news.com.au/entertainment/movies/top-25-australian-movies-revealed-in-new-poll/news- story/2c7d568d0194f2bba19c-89c5ec712db7

It's taken a decade of hard work to create2 award winning, critically acclaimed wolf creek feature films (Released by village roadshow) and 2 seasons of a TV series (Released by STAN in Australia and POP NETWORK in the US, FOX in the UK), as well as publishing 2 prequel novels (Released by Penguin Publishing) and developing our merchandising line of collectables (in collaboration with Ikon Collectibles).

So this hard-won legacy has been tarnished—as well as the future of Australia's most successful and only horror franchise destroyed.

But—this can all be turned around by getting the allegation into court quickly and clearing your name. If it takes six months, a year, 2 years, the damage to the WOLF CREEK brand will have been irreversible. And final. It will be the end of what began and remains an independent Australian success story of a little movie that could. And more than that, the show and your own popularity was literally becoming bigger than ever and all the companies and individuals involved were poised to continue working hard to deliver what fans of the series craved—Mick Taylor.

Thought some background might be useful.

***

Hi Zadia.

I hope you've been as well as you can be under the circumstances.

Unfortunately I feel as I have no option but to withdraw our invitation for Mr John Jarratt to be a part of the Supanova Comic Con & Gaming expos in Adelaide and Brisbane this November.

We must also stop using the advertising campaign we filmed with him earlier in the year.

While we hold to the values of treating John as innocent until proven guilty, and have loved working with him now for a number of years, there are elements of the public and the media who will seek to harm our event by association if we continue to employ or commercially associate with John. You only have to look online for the number of onslaughts that have decimated people and organisations that have tried to stand against that tide.

I hope and pray that the charges are indeed false for both parties—after all its better even for her if she's proven to be a liar rather than the victim of a crime— and that a public so quick to condemn will also be just as willing to reembrace John when that day comes. And may that day come quickly.

***

1 September 2018
RE: National Asbestos Awareness Ambassadorship

Dear John,

It is with deep regret and sadness that I write to inform you that we have been instructed by NSW Government representatives that fund the National Asbestos Awareness Campaign, to advise that your services as a Campaign Ambassador are no longer required due to the charges laid against you.

When the Daily Telegraph's article by Jonathon Moran 'Wolf Creek star John Jarratt is accused of sexually assaulting a woman in the 1970s' was published on the 18 November 2017, we were asked to remove all reference to you as campaign Ambassador on the asbestosawarenes.com.au website.

As Campaign Managers, having worked very closely with you in your role as Asbestos Awareness Ambassador since October 2012, we were extremely confident that the situation would be resolved and strongly recommended that the Committee reconsider this drastic step as no charges had been laid.

At the time we were grateful that the Committee responded favourably to our recommendation. However, when police issued the Future Court Attendance Notice for the offence of rape on 25 August 2018 as published by news.com.au, we were directed to remove all mention of you from the asbestosawareness.com.au website and campaign collateral, which we were compelled to do.

John, it has been an incredible honour to work with you over the past six years in what has been accredited as the world-leading asbestos awareness and education campaign, with much of this success being as a direct outcome of your involvement and support. We have and will continue to hold the greatest respect and admiration for you as a gentleman and a highly skilled professional who has dedicated extensive time and energy while generously lending your internationally acclaimed brand and reputation free of charge, for the single purpose of saving lives.

We hope you will accept our sincere gratitude for all you have done to support the Campaign and increase awareness of the dangers of asbestos among Australian homeowners and tradespersons. While we will never know how many lives have been saved as a result of your kindness and dedication to this purpose, we do know that because of your efforts, there will be many.

We wish you every success in the fight to clear your name and sincerely hope this outcome is forthcoming in the very near future.

A NEW YEAR

I'm actually doing interviews about this tyranny of injustice. I'm being filmed doing this, literally typing while filming *60 Minutes*. I haven't written anything since December 2018. Now is as good a time as any to write of the six months leading up to the trial. I got a voice mail from Gerard O'dwyer, who's playing the lead in *What About Sal?* He's a Down Syndrome man. Below is his voice message from 1 January 2019, word for word. He calls me Terry, the character I played in *McCloud's Daughters*, which he loves.

> Mister John Jarratt, or should I say Terry, how's it going? Merry Christmas and Happy New Year to you and to Rosa and to the family and all the best for 2019. I'm sorry to hear... I'm sorry to hear that you are on trial, I'm sorry to hear that. I saw the newspaper article. I'm sorry that happened to you. Don't let them bully you. Just tell them this is Gerard O'dwyer here, the actor doing a film with you if we get the money and I will stand by you. So um hopefully I'll be um at your side and I will support you, on your behalf. Yeah. Ah, take care Terry... Bye.

After hearing that message I cried and said to Rosa: 'I'm going to do the bloody movie!' I then went to the calendar. 'I'm going to start shooting on 22 April and finish on 25 May'. She asked how I was going to get it together with the rape charge hanging over my head. I told her I didn't know.

It was the best thing I could have done; I went into production mode. I rang Gerard straight away and arranged to meet him and his mum, Anne, in Parramatta for coffee. We sat down in front of some flat whites and I told them I was going to make the movie on 22 April. They said: 'How?' I said: 'I don't know yet'.

I had written the script for *What About Sal?* a few years earlier. It was to be my next project in 2017. The first thing I did was to go through the script and tidy a few things. When I was happy with it I rang my cast members.

When I write, I quite often have someone in mind; this helps because a screen actor looks for authenticity and if I write for one in particular I'll include a lot of who the actor is into the character development. So my cast had been well aware of *What About Sal?* for about three years. I asked them if they were willing and available to do the film for no pay in April/May. They all said yes without hesitation. I then rang the crew who also agreed to do the film for nothing, including gear and facilities.

I was very humbled; totally blown away.

By February 2019 I had the best cast and crew, gear and facilities. Cinematographer Nick A'Hearn and I have two Black Magic cameras, 4k and a 4.6, most lenses, camera gear, lighting, sound and a state-of-the- art post-production facility at Nick's place, where we can develop, pre-produce, produce, post-produce and deliver film, TV, you name it. Why did I have to go to all this trouble and get people to work for nothing? Two reasons: one, they're on my side and, two, investors and funding bodies won't touch me until after the trial. Buggered if I was going to let that stop me.

Next I had to get my amazing producer Kris Maric to organise contracts, budgets, insurances; all sorts of essential details. My first assistant director Mike 'Baba' Faranda and I had to nut out a schedule, and production manager Zadia Jarratt had to sort out the logistics of five weeks' filming. Then she and I and location manager Chris Wheeler had to sort out locations in the north, west and east of Sydney.

Some cast and crew were flying in from Melbourne, Adelaide, Brisbane and the Gold Coast, and we had to organise accommodation, transport and catering. A movie crew had to be wheeled around Sydney for five weeks, plus two weeks of pre-production. On top of that there were legals and insurances, which can't be done for nothing. We needed $100,000 to cover the costs on the ground.

Suddenly it was mid-March 2019. For ten glorious weeks I'd lived in the world I once was in before November 2017. I didn't have time to mope about groundhog day, thinking about rape accusations. That's the thing. If they hadn't taken away my employment by hanging me out to dry in the media, I would have survived ninety per cent better.

It became obvious that somehow we had to raise $100,000. If I wasn't an alleged rapist this wouldn't be a problem. We have a hunch that most Australians don't think I'm guilty so we thought a GoFundMe campaign might work. Being a techno-peasant, I rang my son Charlie. He and I were in a short film *Hero*, put together by three very talented, ambitious young men, Kerryn, Justin and Chad of Taipan Films. He told me to call them as they are much more techno-savvy than me. It was a brilliant move. They had the GoFundMe campaign up and running in no time, plus they shot about twenty promotional videos of Gerard and me. They are hungry young film makers and are now an important part of our future productions, thanks to Charlie.

Unfortunately, the black halo of trial by media has influenced Australians and the GoFundMe campaign is well behind our target. We had to postpone the film to a month after my July trial, so instead of being one week away from starting *What About Sal?* we're sixteen weeks away. For four of those weeks the law would have found me innocent and that will make it much easier to raise the $100,000.

On 1 April I had to ring my cast and crew to tell them the film was postponed to August. They all understood and thought it was actually better to have more time. They are all still on board, God bless 'em.

I had wanted to walk out of court in July and when asked by the media if I was going back to work I'd have answered: 'Already back, just finished appearing in a film which I also wrote, produced and directed'. Now I'll have to say: 'I'm about to... '

I had bitten off more than I could chew. I have this book, my doco, *What About Sal?*, my film doco and *Sixty Minutes*. The film was full on, the other things I can do just plodding along. I've also got to prepare for the trial.

From the 2 April, the heat of organising the film was off and I was back in my head and back in house arrest. Again, I have time on my hands, and the rape allegation gets into my head and won't go away. But this time it's different. I don't want to curl up on the lounge any more, and I don't feel so sorry for myself. I'm bored with it, just fucking sick of it. It used to be such a relief and a release to cry, now I can't be bothered.

Three months feels like 300 years. This is day 515—515 groundhog days—seventy-seven days remaining. All up 592 days!

One day is just rolling into another. For the first time in a long time I really have nothing to do.

But a writer friend of mine Suzy Jarratt (no relation) agreed to do an initial edit of my manuscript. We had a very fruitful meeting on her property in Sydney's northwest. She suggested I let her have a good go at it and then return the words to me. I left feeling a lot more at ease about the book. I couldn't wait to see what she'd do with it.

My son Charlie wanted me to go down for a week and help him work on his new house just west of Melbourne. He and his wife Maddie had saved up and bought their dream house. Not an easy thing to do these days and I'm very proud of them. It's such a blast when you're a dad and you can help your kids in their own homes.

I've built fifteen houses in my time. The fun and camaraderie is exceptional when working with your children. A couple of years before, I did the same with Ebony, and my son-in-law Daniel at their house in Alice Springs.

There are only three things I can't live without: my wife, my children and my grandchildren. In the past I've handled losing my grandparents, my parents, uncles, aunts and some friends. I could not handle losing my wife or kids—I would rather die.

Charlie and I had a ball working together on his house. We would laugh, joke and swap yarns on the way to Bunnings. My life had become so predictable and my stay with Charlie was a wonderful distraction from the nightmare. He is 6' 2", over 100 kilos of blood and muscle, is very bright and he really cares. He would do anything for me— he is my friend. And I have another five just like him; he just happens to be the biggest. My wife and my kids have picked me up and carried me through this nightmare for nearly two years and I know they will never let me down. Just as I will never let them down.

Suzy sent me her edit on this book, it was bloody brilliant. (Joke: she didn't edit that bit.)

I started out as a hack and she's turning me into a writer. The book is easier to follow and it's making much more sense. I hope you're feeling the same way!

It's the beginning of June, four weeks before the trial. The light at the end of the tunnel is shining now. The day is finally coming when I will be free. I'm about to start prepping with my lawyers. The trapdoor from this hole in which I've been living is slowly opening and I can see the sky—it's blue and very bright.

This is my story from the beginning in November 2017 through to 30 June 2019, the day before the trial. Because I was forced into this predicament and publicly shamed for something I didn't do, I felt I should become aware of the sexual atrocities that I and some of my colleagues had been accused of. I needed to educate myself about things I knew very little about and fight for exoneration.

My nose has been stuck in Google, educating myself about the world of sexual assault, indecent behaviour, human and animal behaviour, sex, drugs and alcohol. The involvement of the law, the judiciary and the media. The logical, the illogical, the fairness, the unfairness.

The following chapters are my take on it all, the findings of an amateur investigator. Why? I don't know: all I know is I've been forced into this situation through no fault of my own. It's by far the worst thing that's ever happened to me. Maybe the positive is that I've also been forced to make some sense of it and somehow make some changes through what I've learned, perhaps to make it better in the future for any innocent person wrongly treated or accused. At least it might start a decent productive conversation.

RAPE, PAEDOPHILIA, MURDER: A TRIO OF EVIL

'Accused of rape', 'alleged rapist', 'charged with rape'. I'm sick of the word rape!

It has followed me around like a filthy cockroach for over a year now. I've tried to get rid of it but it just crawls under a cupboard and keeps coming out. Every day, at some point I'm forced to face the ugly thing.

John Jarratt 13, 1965 school photo

When I was 13, I was dragged into the bushes by a big, tall, mature 18-year-old. He raped me. It tortured me for seven years. Then something wonderful happened. When I was 20, Dad got me a job near Townsville during the summer break from NIDA. My dad worked in heavy construction on projects such as the Snowy Mountains Scheme and the North Queensland Beef Roads. The job I had was boring into a rock face with an air-leg, constructing a train tunnel for a copper mine.

Every Friday afternoon my workmates and I would have a few beers at a pub in Townsville. I was 6' 1", 85 kilos, played rugby league and was an amateur boxer. My brother, Brian, was a Golden Gloves runner-up. I could hold my own with him. One Friday I looked down the bar and what I saw horrified me... the man who had raped me.

I went straight up to him and said, 'Remember me?' Suddenly the look of recognition washed across his face and the next instant blood washed across it. I'd punched in his nose, followed by the rest of his head. My workmates had to drag me away.

Belting that maggot made me feel much better. I felt I'd expunged the incident from the torture zone of my heart. Since then it has never got me down until now! It keeps coming up: 'I've never raped anybody, but I've been raped'.

I'm not at all homophobic. Many who've supported me through this are my gay mates, men and women. But I'm repulsed by male genitalia, and watching porn doesn't do it for me. Visions of aroused male genitalia remind me of the lowlife who raped me.

Now I've been accused of the thing I hate the most. Since I've been forced into this nightmare, I've spent a lot of time trying to analyse it. I'm no expert, so this is just my considered opinion after reading, studying and trying to understand.

I call rapists and paedophiles male maggots. They don't deserve to be called men; they're much lower than us. I'd say 99.999% of rapists and paedophiles are males. Where are all the paedophile nuns? I rest my case.

The experts say it's about power. Most people who abuse power are gutless. Some of these selfish little bastards are given the power in the form of millions of dollars from daddy, and become leaders of entire countries. These are the types who rape and grope women. But power in the right hands is a beautiful thing—Oprah, Mandela, Branson, Gates.

Maybe it's about powerlessness as well. People on drugs and alcohol, too down and out to be attractive to a woman, so they stalk her, overpower and rape her. I think they're weak-willed bastards who wake up in the morning and don't give a shit about doing the wrong thing. They want instant gratification. If they can't afford it, they steal it; if they can't attract a woman, they'll rape one. If we decent people really want something, we'll work for it. It might take a few years, but that's what we do.

What's with Catholic priests and ISIS? Priests using their church to cover for raping children, mainly boys. ISIS, in the name of Allah, taking a city, maiming and killing its people, then raping as many women as they can find. Giving themselves to God and, at the same time, holding the devil. If there's a hell, that's where they're going.

I was raised in the country in the 1950s and 60s. If you grabbed a girl inappropriately or said something inappropriate, some other bloke would have a go at you and maybe punch you. Could be your best mate. If you raped someone you wouldn't spend your life in prison, you'd spend it in hospital.

In my teens I was in a little town called Aramac, in outback Queensland, miles from anywhere. There was no TV, so every weekend we'd go to an outdoor movie theatre. We watched a lot of John Wayne westerns. One Saturday night in late 1967, my girlfriend and I left the theatre and went up to the public pool in the park. Not many people were there and it was dark. The trick was to short out the lights so you could play up. We stripped down to our undies and jumped into the pool. I lost my virginity that night. I didn't make love again until a year later with another girlfriend.

In 1969, I moved to Townsville in far North Queensland for my final two years of high school. It was the biggest town I'd ever lived in. I met people there who are still my best mates now. It was a wonderful bunch of mad teenagers, but we were still country people and we had respect for each other. Our social lives were great. We had what's known as good, clean fun.

After high school I auditioned for drama school, NIDA, and I got in. I was somewhat shocked by it all. Guys had long hair, people were smoking dope and taking a lot of drugs and booze. The Beatles were old hat already and Led Zeppelin and Deep Purple were all the go. Woodstock was on everyone's lips. Sex, drugs, rock'n'roll. Naked men and woman swimming in muddy ponds. Love-ins—groovy, man.

I feel that this is when society changed. In many ways for the better—love, peace and the feminist movement. But in other ways, the changes were not so good. Sex became too casual and easy. I think it's turned around and bitten us all on the bum. I'm not talking about rape here, but what I call 'groping and gutter talk'. And it's not exclusive to men, women do it, too. The testosterone in men makes them more predominant. I would guess about a 70/30 differential.

In the 70s I witnessed women walk up to men at parties, grab them by the arm, tell them they want to fuck them, drag them into a room and do just that. I've been grabbed by the balls a number of times over the years, by women and two gay guys—all were unwanted and unsolicited. I think it's disgusting. I was at a movie premiere in 2015 and this drunken, unattractive woman wanted a selfie with me. I was wearing light cotton trousers and she stuck her finger right up my arse. I had her thrown out of the venue. Last year at Supanova, a woman announced she was going to grab me by the bum and did so. This grubby behaviour needs to stop. To touch someone intimately you must earn it, not steal it.

SEX DRIVE

So here's my take on testosterone. It may not be scientifically correct, but I think it's logical. We are mammals. When a mammal comes into season, like a bison, an elephant or a goat, the males fight. The two alpha males, full of testosterone, go into a vicious battle that ends in defeat or death for the vanquished. The victor inseminates the herd or the pack. This happens year in, year out. The aggression and the insatiable appetite among male mammals during rutting season are evident.

But most humans don't behave like that because we have advanced consciousness, reason and communication skills. We know right from wrong. We are aware if we do the wrong thing and it involves others, they're going to get hurt, mentally, physically, spiritually or all three.

When do men and women usually carry on like animals on heat? A large proportion of men and women behave promiscuously when they're drunk. Testosterone goes up and inhibitions come down.

The number of times alcohol is involved in rapes is frightening. Alcohol is, in my opinion, the most aggressive, dangerous drug on the planet. If people who get drunk all the time try to justify it because they really like alcohol, they're lying. They like the feeling of getting drunk. The overall feeling isn't to just 'get happy'. Getting drunk makes you excited and want to be outrageous. A lot of the time it doesn't end in 'happy'. A lot of the time it can end in tears, anger, violence and sexual assault. You can have a good time without getting off your face. You can be outrageous without having excessive alcohol. I guarantee it. I haven't had a drink for thirty years and I can party with the best of them. Drunkenness is a big problem. How many women have to be raped and bashed, how many men have to be king hit, how many families have to die in road crash carnage before this alcohol drug is brought under control.

I don't have an answer to rape, paedophilia and male violence towards women and children, because I don't understand it. Maybe it will always be with us. But maybe we can bring a lot of men around with education at school, and with women setting the bar high by coming out more often about abuse they've suffered, especially by reporting it straight away. The sad part of what happened to me is The Female's evil lie frightens legitimate victims of rape from coming forward. She has betrayed her fellow women.

Every rapist's began life as a beautiful baby. Let's look at how we celebrate from childhood to adulthood.

A toddler's party: clowns, balloons, Wiggles music, dancing, eating lollies and cakes.

A kid's party: being superheroes at the skating rink. Spider-man, Batman, Wonder Woman falling off their ice skates with Justin Bieber booming from the speakers.

Graduating from primary school: 12-year-olds dressing like 20-year-olds at a blue light disco, doing their best to look at least 14.

Schoolies on the Gold Coast: scantily clad girls and shirtless boys with brand new tattoos. Eighteen-year-olds off their tiny faces on alcohol and any drugs they can find—often for the first time. Scores will get hurt, one or two may die, many will have sex, and some girls will be sexually assaulted.

Night clubbing: Men and woman in their twenties and thirties. Scores will get hurt, one or two may die, many will have sex, some girls will be sexually assaulted.

There's something terribly wrong with this. Most rapes are the result of a night out at pubs, parties, night clubs, with women being followed or taken advantage of because of drunkenness and hard drugs: the result of going out for a good time.

Maybe not such a good time.

THE FAMOUS FACE —INFAMY OF THE WORST KIND

For a man, the worst crime to be accused of is the rape of a woman or a child. Too many times, rapists also murder their victims to avoid capture. What's worse than sexual assault and murder—nothing. I can honestly say, I cannot think of worse crimes. Torture, you may say? Viciously raping someone is also first-degree torture. To be accused of sexual degradation is the bottom of the barrel.

To go on television and spend half an hour accusing a well-known person of sexual harassment is very serious. You are accusing them of the worst crime in the eyes of the public, let alone the law. The trouble is, the poor bastard has to wear it as he (usually) can't defend himself and prove his innocence in court if the accusations aren't put before the law. No, it's put before the sleaziest format possible—the media.

Before the advent of the #MeToo movement and the recent popularity of entertainers accusing entertainers about sexual deviancy, those in the early 2000s were outed about addiction, easily the most prevalent offence in the entertainment industry.

The following are just a few well-knowns addicted to drugs or alcohol in the last twenty years, before the #MeToo movement took off.

Drugs: Britney Spears, Robert Downey Jnr, River Phoenix, Heath Ledger, Philip Seymour Hoffman, Michael Jackson, Robin Williams, Amy Winehouse.

Alcohol: Bradley Cooper, Daniel Radcliffe, Carrie Fisher, Lindsay Lohan, Charlie Sheen.

And on and on it goes, I could easily fill two pages with names of entertainers addicted to all sorts of substances.

We all know about them because they're well known and have been outed.

We have more tolerance with addictive crime, because it's nowhere near as bad as sexual crime. Still, you shouldn't be outed just because you're a public figure. It's not freedom of speech, it's exploitation. A well-known drunk being accused of swearing at his teenage daughter and getting sprung will be embarrassing, but it probably won't ruin his career. Sexual slander will ruin your life and your career. Which is fine if you're guilty, inexcusable if you're not.

When I was in my early twenties I was making a film. In one particular scene I was in pyjamas sitting on a chair beside a female actor in a bed. They'd filmed her close up and they were doing the reverse single on me. She was off- camera feeding me lines. Halfway through the scene she placed her hand on my penis. It was out of shot. I somehow kept my cool, finished the scene then quietly asked her what she was doing.

'You loved it' she replied.

'No I fucking didn't,' I said.

This actor was in her early thirties and very well known back in the day. She's well into her seventies now and doesn't get much work these days. I was telling an old mate of mine this story (he's in the business). I didn't mention who it was and when I finished he straight away came up with her name. She had a reputation.

Today I'd have no trouble turning that story into a media storm and making life even tougher for this actor. But why would I do that?

I quite often tell a story about my early days at NIDA, because I think it's funny. In today's world it's interpreted as harassment.

The first year at NIDA, 1971. A very effeminate gay guy used to tease me. He'd always get a reaction from me, the North Queensland country boy who, as far as he knew, hadn't seen a gay person before. He had a habit of sneaking up, wrapping his arms around me and kissing me. I was repulsed by it and he got a kick out of my reaction. I couldn't hit him—it would be like hitting a girl and he knew it.

One night we NIDA students were serving food and wine at a Sydney Theatre Company function. I was carrying a tray full of glasses of white wine. This guy was heading back to the kitchen with an empty tray and took the opportunity to kiss me hungrily on the mouth and there was nothing I could do about it. That was it, I'd had enough!

At that time I was playing rugby league for the University of NSW. On Monday morning I arrived at NIDA with a football under my arm. I found the guy under the fig trees with other students, I walked up and informed him of my plan.

'At lunch time today we're going to the oval for male contact. There will be half an hour of kissing and cuddling, your choice of male contact, and half an hour of football, my choice of male contact. As you've already shown me your male contact, I think it's only fair that I demonstrate mine.'

I gave him the football and then spear tackled him headfirst into the dirt. He started to cry and the other students were very angry with me. I told him there'd be half an hour of that. He never bothered me again. It was sexual harassment. If he did that to me today would I report him? No, I'd spear tackle him into the dirt.

Many prominent men have been outed in recent years for various sexually inappropriate behaviours. Unlike me, at the time of writing, Kevin Spacey and Harvey Weinstein haven't been charged. Unlike me, many people have come out accusing them of sexual harassment. No one has come out about me except the liar, The Female, because there was never anything to accuse me of in the first place.

I can think of four sexual predators who've been jailed in recent times—Robert Hughes from *Hey Dad*, Rolf Harris, Bill Cosby and Larry Nassar. 'Who's Nassar?' I hear you ask. He's the worst of them, but he's not well known. He was the USA Women's Gymnastic doctor who was sentenced to 350 years imprisonment for abusing over 250 women and girls.

Most well-known men who've been outed have only been accused by the media, not in a court of law. Of the allegations that have been made to the police, very few of those accused have been charged and found guilty. But their lives and careers have been ruined and their families have mud all over them. These men can't prove their innocence because they aren't charged. A lot of their accusers haven't gone to the police, but only to the media. The accused men have no recourse. That is unfair. If it's bad enough for a woman to go on a current affairs show and denigrate the bejesus out of a well-known man, then she should take her accusations to the police.

There's a US comedian called Aziz Ansari. He took a woman home and she apparently felt it was 'bad' sex and felt violated. It wasn't bad enough to take to the police but she felt justified in taking it to the media. This is classic 'he said, she said' stuff. If it was bad enough she should have taken it to the police as sexual assault. Why did she take it to the media? Because he's famous! He may or may not have acted inappropriately but we'll never know because it was never investigated. He's now known as a pervert comedian and there's not much he can do about it.

Amy Schumer knows Aziz and her comments lean heavily towards the female. I feel it should be middle of the road. Amy expects better from men and their sexual behaviour these days.

Before the #MeToo movement was in full swing, Amy Schumer didn't pull her verbal punches.

At the *Charlie Sheen Roast*, Amy Schumer spoke about Mike Tyson: 'Look at that face, it's so dark and wrinkly and constantly being pounded it's like Patrice O'Neale's grandmother's arsehole after a gospel brunch.'

I wonder what they'd think of Aziz if he'd said that about the woman who complained about him to the media?

Phoebe Waller-Bridge, the star of a solo play that became a TV series, *Fleabag* (2016–19) and created and wrote the hit TV series, *Killing Eve* (2018–19) went on the Graham Norton Show (18 May 2018) and talked about flashing her 'arsehole' from the wings at a male actor on stage. Absolute proof she acted indecently.
At this very moment her career is going gangbusters with *Fleabag* on Broadway.

Australian actor Craig McLachlan was accused of indecent behaviour in January 2018. He was immediately sacked from the *Rocky Horror Show*, a musical he's been a part of since 1992. He was the producer of the Dr Blake series and single-handedly sold it to Channel 7 when the ABC dropped it. An independent inquiry into his behaviour on *Dr Blake* resulted in his being totally exonerated. But he was dropped from the series and since then he hasn't been employed on screen or in the theatre.

Good thing he didn't go on Graham Norton and say he'd flashed his arsehole at an actor. God knows what they would have done to him.

So it's time for men and women to respect each other more. I've never been a great admirer of filthy comedy. I'm a Seinfeld fan. He's amazingly funny without being disgusting. Australian comedian, Jim Jefferies, can get disgusting. I absolutely love his take on US gun control. He's famous for it—it's not filthy. My take, you don't have to be filthy to be funny. I'm not a fan of gutter talk but maybe I'm old fashioned.

IT TAKES ALL TYPES

When it comes to sexual or violent indiscretions I think there are two types. Again this is just my opinion and I hope you'll agree that it makes sense.

Type 1: Rapists, paedophiles and perpetrators of domestic violence; 99.99% males. Worst crimes on the planet. If a male bashes the bejesus out of a woman or a child, throw away the key. If a male rapes a woman or child, death is too good for them—may they live a life of the most horrific hell on earth. Some say it's about power. I don't think males only do it because they have the physical power. Nuns have the power to rape a child, but it's the priests in their thousands who do it.

Type 2: Gropers and gutter talk. Men and women are guilty of this. As I've mentioned earlier, I've been groped and prodded by women all my adult life and I know plenty of other men who've had similar experiences. But most definitely more women than men are victims of this. Funnily enough, I walked past the TV two days ago and there was a report on this very subject. A survey of victims of groping or gutter talk in the workplace came up with 65% women and 35% men. My gut feeling was 70/30, which wasn't far out.

I believe that the Type 2 problem can be handled with a little more care. Especially if it's a 'she said, he said' situation with little or no evidence. Recently, in separate incidents, a man and a woman in the Labor Party were accused of inappropriate behaviour. They are both proceeding with defamation claims. If they are found to be in the wrong, fair enough but, until that time, they are presumed innocent. Both have had to resign and their careers, established over many years, have been destroyed. If they weren't well known, they'd still be working.

Type 2 shouldn't be seen as women finally punishing men for their dirty deeds as women are guilty of this, too. I agree, of course, that this behaviour has to change for both sexes. Just because women do it less doesn't make the assault less.

As a supporter of the #MeToo movement, I think we should talk about Type 2 in terms of men and women. Men get singled out as if they are always the ones in the wrong in a 'he said, she said' situation. The insinuation is that they are finally learning a good lesson. A number of women need to learn that lesson too. Groping and gutter talk are disgusting and should stop, but are nowhere near as evil as rape and paedophilia. A woman or a man who says, 'Hey, spunk, take your top off and show us your hot body' while slapping that person on the arse is a long way from some maggot throwing a woman onto the ground in a back lane and raping her on the bitumen. Let's put this into perspective, people. Unless the Type 2 is that bad you need to take it to the cops, take your problem to the person involved and try to sort it out. If that's too hard, take it to your boss or board of directors, or trusted friends or family. Don't take it to the media, especially if that person is well known. If you take your problem to the police, let them sort it; again, if you're accusing someone well known don't go to the media until the person is found guilty.

We all have the presumption of innocence: it's the law, and it's everyone's right.

If you don't go to the cops, but you do go to the media, you are no longer just the alleged victim, you've become the sole member of the jury at the trial-by-media court, and you've pronounced the person's guilt while he or she can't defend themselves. It isn't right.

What can we do?

Alcohol: Headlines in the newspapers involve men (usually) off their heads, driving a truck into a motel, glassing someone in the face or urinating off a hotel balcony, killing someone with a king hit outside a club, raping a barmaid in a park on her way home, or belting their wife after a night out. They're never off their heads on marijuana; it's always off their heads on alcohol.

Case in point: A bunch of men drunk off their heads: 'Let's start a fight!' A bunch of men stoned off their heads: 'Let's start a band!'

When a rape or a bashing takes place, most of the time, excessive use of alcohol is involved. Sure, drugs like ice and heroin are dangerous, too, but they aren't sold at a bar or in a bottle shop like alcohol. Litres of it, as much as you can drink, no limits unless you're driving.

Driving under the influence of alcohol is a serious offence. Random Breath Testing was implemented in the mid-1970s in Australia. We were all made aware through national campaigns that drink driving was extremely dangerous. Your car became a weapon and if you were drunk and ran into someone and killed them, you were a murderer. I took this very seriously. I was never a frequenter of bars, pubs or nightclubs. I didn't drink that much, but when I did, I got drunk very quickly. I was a two-bob drunk. If I went to a party in my car and drank too much, I'd get a cab home.

My father drummed into me, 'A cab fare is much cheaper than a jail sentence and a murder on your hands'. That got through to me. I've never been arrested for drunkenness... I've never been arrested for anything. The closest I've come to it was on Scotland Island in 1980. A do-gooder neighbour noticed I had a marijuana plant growing in my backyard. Because he told the poor old cops they had to act on it. I got fined. This bastard put people in for everything, even illegal chook pens. It got so bad the woman who was his next door neighbour lost it one day and had an all-in fight with him. She won. It was a good day on the island.

The ban on drink driving has been very successful, with fewer people severely injured and many lives saved. A lot of people love a drink and do so sensibly; my brother Brian is one of them. He loves a beer on the weekend, but he knows when to stop. He doesn't throw up on the bar or get falling-down drunk. He likes to get to the point where he's merry and having a good time. Not all of us can do that. I gave up because being an occasional drinker wasn't safe for me. I'm a binger, full stop. I rarely buy my favourite thing—dark chocolate-coated macadamias. Even with my greatest efforts, I'll eat the whole packet in front of the TV knowing I'm being weak and indulgent. So I know how hard it is. I'm strong because I'm weak. Like a lot of people, it took me years to work that out.

Some people have control. Mum liked an occasional drink but never got drunk once. She loved a glass or two of port with friends or family but would get to a point where she'd stop: 'No more for me thanks, I'm getting a bit tiddly'.

I think that's the point all drinkers should get to. I'm not being a wowser when I say getting drop-down drunk is disgusting and it shouldn't be allowed. To an extent that's already happening. If someone's deemed to be too drunk, barkeepers can refuse to serve them.

Society recognised the tremendous problem we have with drunk driving. We put a lot of effort into not driving drunk, and we should apply the same effort into protecting our youth against physical violence in all its forms, especially when they're out trying to have a good time. Kids want to enjoy their lives, not destroy their lives.

At the moment, people leave nightclubs at 1 or 2am. Most of them are off their faces. Anything and everything happens at this point.

Men and women falling into gutters, arguments and fist fights. A drunken male looking at a collapsed woman with her skirt up to her waist, legs apart and showing her knickers is easy prey. This maggot picks her up and walks her home. She is so drunk she blacks out and later wakes up in a park without her knickers, and wondering how the hell she got there.

I'm not making up this scenario, and it's not unusual. But if this bloke and the woman had separately been kicked out of the club earlier in the night when they'd had too much to drink, this incident might never have occurred.

Getting really drunk is unacceptable. It's so bloody dangerous on every level—the big three again: mentally, physically, spiritually. Being a boring old granddad doesn't make it easier. Four of my six children went to schoolies—two to go. One of my sons rang me, drunk as a skunk, informing me he was being 'inked'. He was getting a tattoo.

Education

Even the plainest babies have a cuteness about them. Not being the most beautiful baby doesn't take away their wonderment, their innocence, their purity. How do babies go from that to Adolph Hitler, Charles Manson or Larry Nassar?

Education is essential. I think 'How to lead a decent life' should be on the curriculum. If you're nine-to-fiving every day you average thirty-five hours of work time and ninety-three of personal time.

Schools prepare you to acquire a job, trade or a career to make the money on which you can live. But they don't teach *how* to live.

We're not taught about how to express emotion, how to grow or how to change. Schools don't teach what's acceptable, when to compromise, how to treat people, how to stay positive and contented. I could go on forever. These are far-reaching subjects and, just like maths and English, they should be compulsory.

We could at least have an expert touring schools and pointing out that, at one time in their lives, sexual offenders went to school. Wouldn't it be a good idea to state to the children: 'In this class there could be a potential rapist or paedophile. In a few years' time you may be about to rape a helpless woman or child—remember this day and stop. Banish those thoughts—seek help.'

If you become a drunk, your chances of sexually abusing women and children jumps exponentially, as does the risk of your murdering someone or beating the shit out of your wife and kids.

Be a man, not a maggot.

In Australia alone, on average, one woman a week is killed from domestic violence. Here's an idea... instead of Kim Kardashian's bum and boobs, once a month put up the faces of the women who've been murdered on the front page.

THE TIMES THEY ARE A CHANGIN'

By the mid-60s, Frank Sinatra and Dean Martin were middle-aged crooners. Elvis Presley, The Beach Boys, Aretha Franklin, Tina Turner, The Beatles, The Rolling Stones, Janis Joplin, Joe Cocker and Tom Jones had arrived to take their place. Sex, drugs and rock 'n' roll. For the first time, women were on the pill and men were looking for the G-spot. Unreal, far out, groovy, man.

Marijuana, tripping, cushions, bean bags, tie-dyed parachute drapes and 'Stairway to Heaven' at two in the morning, love-ins. Is this a dream? Have I died and gone to heaven?

This boy from Townsville was in swingin' Sydney.

The 70s and 80s were off the planet. Free love! Men and women were at it. The touching and feeling between them made today's claims of sexual misbehaviour look tame. Again, men were the prominent touchers and feelers, but women did their fair share. I'm not going to mention names in this book, because that is the problem. I'm not going to ruin anyone's life or career unless that person is a convicted rapist or paedophile.

I could tell you of many incidents involving famous men, but that seems to be well documented lately. There's an Australian actor who's my age who used to tweak your balls by way of saying hello. She was well known for it. Funnily enough, she was considered a 'ballsy' actor—still is.

In 1979, when I was doing *The Last Outlaw*, another actor, who's still a close friend of mine, came into a crowded room, drunk, grabbed one of the leading actors and said, 'Let's fuck,' as she dragged him into the nearest bedroom.

I was at an awards night after-party in the 1980s standing with another two actors. She thought it was funny to reach across and squeeze his balls. He wasn't amused.

In the mid-80s the dreaded AIDS arrived. In the entertainment industry we lost a lot of wonderful, talented people, including one of my best friends and Australia's greatest actor, John Hargreaves. Casual sex was over; we all had to behave ourselves.

Look, this isn't an excuse, there is no excuse for dirty talk and groping. I could easily out the well-known actors mentioned above and talk about them on the ABC, but I don't think it's fair.

In 1981 I was on *We of the Never Never*. A group of us were in the bar. A woman who worked with the art department, casually came up and seductively stroked my penis and wanted me to go to her room. I told her to piss off. Now, even if I wanted to, I couldn't out her, because she is not well known, so there's no way I could ruin her career. That is why male celebrities should be outed privately for groping, not publicly unless it is out-and-out sexual assault. Again, if it's that bad, take it to the cops. If that man is charged and stands trial, only on court day should he be outed if found guilty.

Double standards

I was with my teenage son at Manly Beach in the summer of 2016. Women were walking past in very skimpy bikinis; the bottoms were like G-strings and the tops just covered their breasts. My son said: 'Hey, Dad, if women don't want to be sex objects how come they dress as objects of sex?'

I couldn't put it better myself. In the 1970s women who dressed provocatively were usually hookers and strippers.

While there is no earthly excuse for a man to leer and grope he cannot be condemned for looking at a female in public who is almost naked. Speaking as the father of two daughters, I have to say if you must dress like that on a crowded beach, ensure that when you leave you put on something less provocative that won't incite the attention of a deviant who could do you harm.

Men are twenty times more sexually charged than women, as are the male mammals in nature, but these are only rampantly on heat for two months of the year. Human males are on heat all the time. But this isn't an excuse for unsavoury, degenerate behaviour. However, most men know how to behave themselves, as do most women. But I don't think it's right for a raunchily-dressed female to be up-in-arms if a man looks at her. Just as there's nothing wrong with women looking at Chris Hemsworth with his shirt off.

It's only wrong when it gets gross.

In my day it was Elvis, The Beatles and Tom Jones. Women at their concerts would scream so loudly you couldn't hear the singing. And when Tom Jones performed they would take off their knickers and throw them at him.

Imagine if men took off their underpants and hurled them at Whitney Houston back in the day—there'd be a public outcry!

We humans are strange creatures.

The bottom line is most people are OK. A small percentage of men, and an even smaller percentage of women, are not. A tiny number of men are violent, rapists and/or paedophiles but you don't know this until it's too late. Most men will respect the way women want to dress; a rapist, unfortunately, will take advantage. One degenerate in a crowd of decent men is all it takes. This is the horrible world we live in. As far as I'm concerned women should never be alone in a lonely place. As I tell my daughters, get a cab home, if you're short of money, give me a call, I'll throw some dollars on your credit card.

Men are also twice as strong as women but that doesn't give us the right to punch you in the face. When we read headlines: 'men are violent' or 'men are perverts' it hurts because most of us are not. Please remember to add 'some' to these headlines.

Another one: 'Men against women'. Wrong: most men are married to women and most will say their wives are their best friends. Rosa is most certainly mine. She is my soul mate and the love of my life. Throughout my ordeal, she's been my rock—I would be lost without her.

Actors versus priests

The Catholic Church has a huge problem with its staff. In the United States alone, between 1950 and 2015, 4444 priests were accused of sexual rape of children. Approximately one in ten priests is a paedophile. By the law of averages that means that if 1000 priests are in a room, 100 of them are paedophiles.

Over seven decades in Pennsylvania alone, 300 priests were accused of sexually molesting over 1000 children!

The entertainment industry doesn't have a huge problem with its staff. Internationally from 1895 until now, twenty-eight entertainers have been charged or accused of sexual crimes. Six did time: Bill Cosby (2018). Rolf Harris (2014). Robert Hughes (2014). Gary Glitter (2006). Oscar Wilde (1895).

My point? As mentioned previously, I'm a fully-fledged supporter of the #MeToo movement, which is against sexual harassment and sexual assault, mainly by men. It ranges from unacceptable behaviour to rape, and everything in between. I'm all for it. The movement has made its impression and achieved positive results.

However, certain members of the entertainment industry have been crucified and I'm one of them. In order to try to change things I will just have to wear that.

I applaud that Bill Cosby was hammered and found guilty but others, like Cliff Richard, were savagely maligned and he was innocent. There's nothing good about that.

When an actor outs a famous face from the entertainment industry it's newsworthy. Quite a few have outed Harvey Weinstein. Because of the current climate, the woman's story is usually the one the public believes. I understand that. But when a female accuser becomes an accused, I think the #MeToo movement should hammer her just as hard.

This movement went a bit weird in August 2018. Asia Argento was one of the high-profile actors who claimed Weinstein raped her. Turns out she, too, did a bit of sexual assaulting. Her boyfriend at the time, the late Anthony Bourdain, forked out US$380,000 in hush money to a young man she had seduced when he was 16. You are smart enough to see the hypocrisy and the preposterousness of this. It's a reality check, kids. A signal from the universe that this #MeToo pendulum needs to swing back to the sensible middle ground.

It is supposed to be about women outing men; mostly it has been about women outing men in the entertainment industry and there's a very good reason for that. If you accuse a so-called celebrity you will get widespread media coverage. If, on the other hand, you're a woman working in a big firm and you're locked in an office and assaulted by the boss, it's a different scenario. The woman goes to the police, who investigate the incident. If they find hard evidence of rape it goes to court and he is convicted. The local paper might print a couple of paragraphs on page 16. If he's found innocent, it won't make the papers at all.

But if he is known to the public it will be in all the world's media for months, whether or not he is guilty.

This kind of exploitation must stop now. Too many innocent men have had their lives and careers undeservedly permanently ruined.

TRIAL BY MEDIA

It's a modern day witch hunt. And the accused, even when found innocent, can be forever stigmatised.

For my money, the best actor on the planet today is Australian Geoffrey Rush. I'd pay good money to watch him read the weather report, but because of undergoing a trial by media he may never act again. This is not just sad, it's a tragedy. The two main allegations were that he put his hand on the small of Eryn Jean Norvill's back while waiting to carry her on stage in King Lear and, he brushed her breast while carrying her 'corpse' downstage towards a full house during a preview performance. Norvill was playing Cordelia, the daughter of Lear.

When I play Mick Taylor in a *Wolf Creek* torture scene and there is a break between set ups, I have to stay within the boundaries of my 'full on' character. The Everest of Shakespeare is Lear. An exceptional actor like Geoffrey would be 'in the zone'. He'd be in character, trying to feel the enormity of losing his daughter. When he had a hand on her back it would be to connect Lear to Cordelia. For God's sake, he's about to carry her corpse on stage, consumed with grief and wail in heartbroken agony. I'm quite sure he's not thinking seconds before going on stage, 'Mmm, Eryn's got a nice back'.

Geoffrey's in his 60s and he's not strongly built. How do you carry a dead weight with one arm under her armpit without occasionally brushing the breast?

He was also accused of lewd messages such as, 'I've got a stage door Johnny crush.' Eryn Norvill sent a couple of texts to Rush calling him: 'Galapagos lusty thrust' and 'Jersey cream-filled puff'. Look for them on Google. They're difficult to find, whereas Geoffrey's messages are very easy to locate.

He went on to have a huge win with his defamation case. The *Daily Telegraph* had got the story from some nong at the Sydney Theatre Company who had no right to disclose what was a complaint against Rush by Norvill, who left instructions that it was to remain private. The police had nothing, absolutely nothing, to do with all this. It was completely and utterly media driven with headlines like 'The Geoffrey Rush Trial'. He was never on trial. It was the *Daily Telegraph* that was on trial.

To top it off another actor, Yael Stone, went on the ABC and tore Geoffrey to shreds, accusing him of being perverse. If Stone felt so strongly she should have taken the matter to the police.

If they find that a person has a case to answer the current Australian law allows media to publish that information.

In my view that should only happen if the accused goes to trial. Instead, it seems you can go on TV and say what you bloody like about someone. And immediately the Goggle Box judge and jury begin sitting in judgement.

What can Geoffrey do about it? Nothing. He has a right of reply, but I'll tell you something—if anyone is expecting that people who hear stories of sexual assault (verbal or physical, implied or explicit, weak or strong) will hold their judgement until a verdict in court is reached, you are kidding yourself.

This whole thing is an absolute travesty.

The Australian law

The International Covenant on Civil and Political Rights (ICCPR) protects the presumption of innocence: Everyone charged with a criminal offence shall have the right to be presumed innocent until proved guilty according to the law.

The ICCPR is a multilateral treaty adopted by the United Nations General Assembly.

International instruments cannot be used to 'override clear and valid provisions of Australian national law.'

On Saturday, 18 November 2017 headlines across the nation appeared on all media platforms, 'Wolf Creek Star in Rape Claim', accompanied by a photo of me as the serial killer Mick Taylor. The public recognises the image, the character is known all around this country.

A gossip columnist wrote the following article mentioned below:

> The star of one of Australia's most harrowing horror films has been accused of sexual assault in the wake of Hollywood's Harvey Weinstein scandal.
>
> John Jarratt, pictured above, as *Wolf Creek* villain Mick Taylor...

Of course every photograph and film clip used in various media was of me in character as Mick Taylor.

The introduction on the front page mentions 'the star of Australia's most harrowing horror film' and then aligns me with Harvey Weinstein. Don't you think this kind of reporting puts me in a bad light? This is against the law.

In this country I have the right to be presumed innocent until proved guilty according to the law.

The media has covered me in a veil of guilt with the connection to the *Wolf Creek* character. The Female isn't mentioned by name, as she has a suppression order to protect her presumption of innocence. Where's mine?

This same story pops up whenever I go to court—there have been five court hearings so far, one to go!

In 2017, The Female said the alleged event happened in 1975, making her 18 at the time. Then she worked out she had made a mistake—it was 1976; she was nearly 20 and I was nearly 24. But the media didn't revise her age, continuing to refer to her as an 18-year-old. It doesn't sound much but '18 just past 17' is creepier than '19 nearly 20.' In other articles, they've described her as 'a teenager', implying I'm also a paedophile.

Being accused of rape in 2017 is bad enough, being charged with rape in 2018 is horrific beyond belief. The media went nuts. As mentioned earlier, journalists at our home ambushed me, my wife, and my mother-in-law. And the Goggle Box jury brayed: 'There's got to be something in it—he's been charged!'

One of my best friends, Linley, when recently visiting her childhood home, was asked by some of her friends if I'd done it. It transpired there are plenty who think I'm in the wrong—disturbing to say the least.

A woman once came up to me and asked: 'Has anyone ever said that you look like John Jarratt?' This happens a lot—some people can't believe I'd be in their neighbourhood. My pat answer is, 'All the time, but I'm taller, better looking and he's fatter than me.'

This woman agreed: 'Yeah, he's an arsehole anyway. Did you read about him?'

More recently, I was in a supermarket getting grapes. A woman walked up and said: 'Keep your eyes to yourself, you filthy pig, I know who you are!'

I stay at home a lot. I don't like being in large crowds at the moment. An island in the South Pacific sounds nice. Can't do it, though, I've got to stick around and fight.

SUPPRESSION ORDER

A suppression order is the act of preventing something from being seen or expressed or from operating.

Mine is a 'she said, he said' case. There is no hard evidence, it's historical, it happened forty-three years ago. If I was caught on CCTV footage sexually assaulting someone and you could definitely recognise my face on camera, then go ahead and put me and the footage on the nightly news straight away. It's hard evidence. I obviously did it.

I'm told by the lawyers that one of the big reason the accused doesn't get a suppression order is that the NSW Police wants the person's name in public so that other possible victims may come forward. This doesn't make sense. In 2018, 26,312 victims of sexual assault came forward. Around about a dozen well-known men have been publicly named as sex offenders. So out of 26,312 alleged sexual offences only about twelve of them were publicly shamed, myself included. So 26,300 accused were unknown and didn't get public attention. Not giving 26,000 sexually accused men suppression orders may bring forward a very small handful of other women victims. It doesn't add up. This is the excuse the police used to hang me on display publicly for two years. By the way, no other women ever came out to accuse me in two years.

They should remove the existing terms 'alleged victim' and 'alleged perpetrator'. The terms used should be 'accuser' and 'accused'. Calling me the alleged perpetrator gives me an aura of guilt and calling The Female the alleged victim gives her an aura of innocence. We both have a presumption of innocence. As it turns out, I'm no longer the alleged perpetrator, I am the victim.

Because The Female is the 'alleged' victim and I'm the 'alleged' perpetrator, she received a suppression order which will stay in place until the trial. Her name has been withheld. Why? Presumed innocent until found otherwise beyond reasonable doubt. We are both presumed innocent. We both should have a suppression order. Now, my 12-year-old granddaughter could see the simple logic in that. What is wrong with the lawmakers? How and why do they allow this obvious anomaly to continue!

As it turns out, I'm innocent and The Female is guilty of lying. If anything, my name should have been withheld and her name revealed... not that it would have greatly affected her as she is not a public identity.

Now I'm no lawyer, but you don't have to be Einstein to deduce that what happened to me is highly illogical and unjustified. My identity should have been withheld simply because Australian law is supposed to protect me and my right to a presumption of innocence. I should not be exposed in any way until the end of the trial when the judge says 'Not guilty'.

I'm going to Canberra about this and I'm not leaving until they legislate for all that I've outlined above. It's too late for me but maybe I can ensure others no longer have their careers ruined by the media.

Most high-profile people are famous for their work. A great politician, an amazing athlete, a brilliant singer, a gifted actor, a genius inventor—the list goes on. If such people are maligned for years by the media before being found innocent, their brilliant careers are ruined or severely compromised and their families vilified. We lose greatly talented people making valuable contributions to society, and we witness their disintegration.

You may say: 'Who cares, they're rich', but for a person who doesn't want to stop what they are doing, being left sitting on a pile of money may as well be a pile of shit.

On the other hand, if that person is found guilty—end of story, start throwing bricks.

The media screams about freedom of speech. OK, that's fine. Unfortunately, freedom of speech is loosely defined. Maybe, when I go to Canberra, we can look at that, too. Like everything in life, say or write whatever you like, but not if it unduly hurts someone or is one-sided.

When you train to become a journalist, the first thing you're taught about reporting is that it must be independent, fair and unbiased.

If I was a journalist I would have written:

> 'Iconic actor accused of a dubious historic sexual assault !'
> A 60-year-old woman has told police that an Australian actor sexually assaulted her in 1976. This actor has strongly denied...'

It's not about freedom of speech it's about ratings and internet hits. It's about degradation, shame, humiliation and indignity. I don't know why the gossip columnist would write such horrid stuff. Because he wants to hurt me? No, he obviously doesn't give a fuck about me or my family. He just wants to tap dance around the office celebrating his scoop.

Freedom of speech has become freedom to ruin lives. Imagine you're a well-known Australian male actor and you're well respected and have the lead in a play. An up-and-coming young actress fantasises about having an affair with you. She's attractive, and you like her, but she comes onto you. You tell her you're happily married and she should back off. She doesn't and in the end you get angry and tell her to fuck off. Five years later she's full of resentment. This actress goes on TV and gives a very good performance about you being a pervert and never leaving her alone. The press takes her side, because it's gold for them. And unfortunately that's what's happening in the #MeToo climate. You have no way of proving your innocence because she hasn't gone to the police.

Finding the above a bit far-fetched? Well, I've got a stalker. I've made sure plenty of people know about her, including my wife. Hopefully that will be enough if she tries to do a job on me. She's not an actor, by the way. If I get my way in Canberra, no one will be able to go on TV and name a well-known person as a sexual pervert. Anyone can be wrongfully accused. I have been and my mission is to right the wrong.

If I was a concreter instead of an actor this is what would have happened:

In November 2017, The Female would have gone to the police and said John the Concreter had raped her. She'd go to the *Daily Telegraph* and the journo would ask: 'John who? Never heard of him, go away'. By about March 2018, the cops would tell me about the 1976 sexual assault. I'd then get a lawyer and after talking to him, go to the police and make a statement. My lawyer would tell me it could take six to eight months for the cops to throw it out. I continue concreting. Apart from my wife nobody, including my kids, would know about it. In August 2018, to my lawyer's amazement, I get charged. In March 2019 I get my trial date, February 2020. I tell my concreting workmates I'll then be taking time off for one week. I don't tell them what for. I go to trial for a week, nobody notices, nobody cares, especially the press. I go back to concreting the following week and nobody knows anything about it! I'm a bit pissed off that the woman did such a thing but look at the bright side.

John the Concreter only lost a week's wages, nobody knew about the allegations and it's all over.

John the Actor lost two years, everybody knew about it and it's not over.

SOLUTIONS

Sexual and violent abuse in the entertainment industry is a problem, but it's a long way from our worst problem. You want to see large numbers? Have a look at our long lists of alcoholics and addicts. Hand-in-hand with all that comes suicide. That is by far our worst problem. Sexual indiscretion looks prolific in my industry because we are called out publicly when it raises its head. Other industries don't have that exposure but that doesn't mean there are fewer serious problems in other workplaces.

A survey taken by Shine lawyers found that the two worst states for sexual harassment were Queensland and the ACT. Most incidents happened in office buildings where generally the perpetrators were male senior staff.

So the most prolific sexual predator is a podgy, middle-aged man in a grey suit who drives a Mercedes and lives in a four-bedroom house with a wife and kids in an inner-city suburb of Brisbane or Canberra. Bloody boring having a bloke from accounts on the front page when you can have the *Wolf Creek* or the *Rocky Horror Show* bloke instead.

A news story about an actor going into rehab is pretty sad. Probably true, but you'd have to say self-inflicted. You feel sorry for him and he may get help and a lot of public sympathy. Unless he keeps turning up off his face, he'd most probably continue to work. Not so for an actor accused of sexual harassment.

There are five ways to really hurt somebody mentally, physically and spiritually. Rape, paedophilia, sexual molestation, murder and violence, especially against women and children. This is as serious as it can get.

If anyone is accused of the above without hard evidence, there should be a suppression order forbidding the use of their name until a court of law issues its verdict.

No one should be able to make public a sexual complaint about another person. It is one person's word against another's. If it's so horrific that you feel the need to ruin his reputation on TV then it's horrific enough to take it to the police, like the women in the Brisbane and Canberra offices have to do. The media isn't interested in those stories.

So this is what I propose:

There should be directly related charges available for false rape accusations, not a charge for false rape accusations under the veil of 'false report of a felony'. Such charges would send the message that no one can destroy an innocent individual's life and get away with it without consequence.

In a 'she said, he said' case with no evidence, and/or a historic case, both parties are presumed innocent and both should be issued with a suppression order. Their names should not be made public until the court decides the outcome.

If a media outlet ignores the suppression order and makes the names public, the journalists responsible should be heavily fined and sacked.

The presumption of innocence remains until the last moment of a trial. Therefore, legally, the trial shouldn't be made public until the decision moment.

Accusing someone of any form of sexual depravity is serious. The accuser needs to take it to the police. If the media goes ahead and names and shames the person, then the accuser should be heavily fined, the media outlet heavily fined and the personnel involved lose their jobs.

If the above were in place, you would not have known about my rape charge until 5 July 2019. All you would have known was that I'd been found innocent of a rape charge. A rape that never happened, not in 1976, not ever.

FROM ROSA'S PERSPECTIVE

The initial shock of this horrendous allegation of rape made against John, a man who is known for his contribution to the Australian entertainment industry as an actor, both here and afar, was dreadful. To falsely accuse a person of a crime is an assault on all one's senses, causing long-lasting trauma. It seeps into every cell of one's being and causes much unnecessary suffering.

Around this time, I came across a quote that spoke to me, from the thirteenth century mystical poet Rumi: 'Sorrow prepares you for joy. It violently sweeps everything out of your house, so that new joy can find space to enter. It shakes the yellow leaves from the bough of your heart, so that fresh, green leaves can grow in their place. It pulls up the rotten roots so that new roots hidden beneath have room to grow, whatever sorrow shakes from your heart, far better things will take their place.' –*Rumi*

I was so humbled and moved to hear of the public outcry offering support for John. It felt like a sea of many arms stretched high in the air, holding up the man, offering their love and support. Beautiful messages, calls, emails, poured in from family, friends, and work colleagues. Everyone that knows the private John would instinctively know, without a doubt, that it is an outrageous lie and that he would never be capable of such vile behaviour. He is a loving and generous husband, father of six children and grandfather to three grandchildren, all with their unique personalities, who all love him dearly.

So much time and energy has been spent navigating through this false allegation: time better spent doing more for the women, men and children living in constant fear suffering from domestic violence and sexual violence, sometimes sadly resulting in death. The amazing courage and strength that it would take to survive and overcome such an experience, and to then light the way for others that are facing the same horror is inspiring.

This anonymous woman, who presents as the victim, is protected by law and stays anonymous unless she chooses to reveal herself. Once her lie is exposed, she still walks free with no accountability or monetary outlay. This woman is known to John and myself and, long ago, we had been on friendly terms for a few years. Turning the spotlight to that time, reveals to me how trusting I was. As a mature woman today, my intuition serves me extremely well. It allows me to paint the scene in my mind and see today, the hidden motives, cunning ways and deceit displayed by this person, long ago, a memory shrouded in secret betrayal.

There is a question that I'm asked quite a lot: 'Why now?' Why indeed!

So let me paint another picture: the young woman did not ride into the sunset with my husband as she had schemed.

John and I remarried in 2016 after being divorced for twenty-seven years. This woman saw her opportunity to inflict her spite, jealousy and greed, to accuse, discredit and destroy the man, his marriage to me, and our family.

I would imagine that in her mind, she would think that she would gain fame and fortune on the back of the #MeToo movement—a movement that in my opinion needs rebalancing, and I'm glad we are having the conversations and starting to seriously address the imbalances. And, by the way, let us remember there are women behaving badly also in this dynamic.

There is an opportunity now for men to speak up as well about their experience of being falsely accused of sexual assault without the shame that comes with it.

In moments when I have felt less Zen, I would imagine this woman receiving a symbolic slap from me to her cheek. This symbolic slap she may well feel when justice is served in court.

From across the world on the island of Sicily, Mt Etna was erupting. It felt like my birthplace was supporting us, and was spitting fire in defiance of this outrageous claim. I shared this with John's lawyer, the unique and charismatic, with a razor-sharp mind, Chris Murphy, which immediately transported him back to some wonderful memories from his time spent holidaying in the Mediterranean. Chris and his legal team, Brian, Daniel, Rose and Daria, have gone beyond, including the amazing Barrister Greg James, believing in John's innocence and standing in support of the man and against the injustice of it all. Our adult children now want to adopt Greg as their new uncle.

The morning the allegation became public, the media was ready to ambush and expose John, while he was working at a large event in Adelaide. Our daughter Zadia, who was working with him on that day, went into protective mode to stop the reporters from having access to her papá. She was finding it hard to breathe, while trying to be strong for her papá, and doing her best to disguise the beginnings of a panic attack. John's son Charlie flew immediately from Melbourne to offer his protection and support to both. The next morning a reporter and a cameraman from Channel 7 appeared on my doorstep, without being invited. I found these experiences to be quite invasive.

The media have been deliberate and cruel in how they have portrayed John. They have not shown him any respect, knowing full well that there are six children and three grandchildren to consider and how it may affect them. The media did not bother to wait until the allegation was fully investigated and processed through a court of law. They have shown a total disregard for a fellow human being, not caring if the allegation is true or false, but just wanting to raise their profiles and fill their pockets. It is disrespectful and irresponsible journalism and reporting.

Another image I will share with you.

The caged man, gagged and bound, suspended in public and exposed for all to see. His spirit broken and rendered powerless to defend his name and protect his family. What happens when the media does this to an innocent man?

The man is publicly stripped of his dignity, shamed, humiliated, denied his livelihood, unable to support his family, unable to feel free.

Sadly, I have been witness to the emotional damage and the downward spiral that has weighed heavily on John, inflicted by the deliberate actions of the media in perpetuating this lie of rape.

Another media frenzy occurred months later, when John was charged. John's legal team were shocked with the DPP's decision to charge him. At this stage the police had done little towards investigating this case. It was at this time that everything intensified tenfold. I could feel the doors shutting quickly around us, affecting us in every way, like a domino effect. This sort of thing brings you to your knees.

Along this journey there have been some wonderful people, each with their special gifts, who have given me valuable insight, support and counsel, for which I will be eternally grateful. Even our ancestors lend support from the heavens. In our bleakest moment an Earth Angel arrives, the blue-eyed one, the one who extends a loving hand and generous heart. Never in my wildest dreams would I have imagined such generosity of spirit. Our hearts are filled with profound gratitude, and we can now breathe easier again.

To the woman who started this terrible lie and to the media who have participated in keeping the lie alive, I say shame on you. I also say, shame on you for exposing our beautiful Jazzie to primary schoolyard harassment. Her parents Daniel and Ebony, along with the school principal, acted swiftly and wisely to stop this in its tracks. She was only 11 years old, too young to be exposed to this. She is a big reason, including our amazing daughters, to raise my voice against this kind of injustice.

I had been working on a painting for the last three months leading up to John's court date, and lay down my brushes the day before the trial was to begin. The painting is titled 'Calm Waters'. It reflects my emotional journey of connecting to my inner calm when surrounded by surreal chaos, and finding the strength and courage within, to go forward with grace and dignity, amidst the harsh spotlight of scandal and judgement. I am extremely pleased to know that in a few months this painting will hang at a tropical paradise retreat.

My experience of the court process, with the addition of photographers and reporters, was chaotic and quite surreal. The outcome of the case was in the hands of the chosen twelve called for jury duty that week. If the woman's lies were believed, John would've faced a five-year jail sentence. By not focusing on this, it allowed us to be stronger in spirit to deal with the drawn-out challenge that we were facing. During the week of the trial, our children came together in full solidarity to offer their love and support for what I know was a terrifying experience for them all.

The atmosphere of a criminal court room is a seriously sombre one. The written law, that is steeped in tradition and ritual, is displayed with great respect, by the judge and barristers adorned in their costumes of red, white and black. The protocol is to stand and bow as the judge enters or leaves the courtroom. The stage is set, the players take their position, knowing their roles, in this theatrical real-life drama, of an event from our private life, that occurred long ago. The seats on the left side of the court room, opposite where family, close friends and supporters were sitting, were occupied by journalists, reporting from their laptops, as the story by all witnesses, including myself, and as the crown witness unfolded each day. These journalists remain very cool and detached, as if an invisible wall separates them from you. It was bizarre to sit beside them knowing they were writing about this woman's lies, writing about our private, personal life.

We waited in heightened anticipation to hear those two magical words, 'Not guilty'! The alternative outcome would've been unbearable suffering and emotional damage to us all, especially John. Our spirits broken beyond repair.

As the not guilty verdict was announced, we all individually experienced this primal cry, rising from deep within us. We gave ourselves permission to exhale this terrifying burden that had been with us for nearly two years. Uncontrollable sobbing, and hugs all round, relieved and so grateful to the jury, the chosen twelve, for their swift, fifteen-minute unanimous decision in John's favour. So grateful to Greg, John's barrister, an absolute angel with a flair for music and theatre, an encyclopedic mind for the law, and a love and great knowledge of history.

We, as a family, have walked fearlessly through the eye of the storm, armed with strength, courage, love, and support. We are now healing from this experience, but it will take some time. We can breathe, freedom is in the air. There is enormous relief and eternal gratitude to all who played their parts for justice to be served.

It has been a heart-opening, transforming experience to go through.

THE TRIAL

The month of June 2019 was put aside to prepare for the trial which was to begin on Monday, 1 July at 10 am.

My lawyers, Chris Murphy and Bryan Wrench, drove me hard. On the first Sunday in June, Bryan made me go through the statements with a fine-toothed comb. Word by word; sentence by sentence. We'd done this so many times before—twenty months of trying to reconstruct what, where, when and how things happened in 1976. Everything was in place. But now here we were going through it again. Surely we couldn't possibly come up with anything new. We did. We always did. If you have his practice, 'Murphy's Law', on your side you have to know everything about everybody involved, every scrap of evidence. A clear recollection about our truth and when and why it happened; and a clear recollection of the other side's story, which parts were mainly lies, and the reasons for them.

Forty-three years ago! 1976! How in God's name can anything be remembered way back then?

I was in the car with Rosa and I asked her a question: 'Earlier this year what month did we visit Rick and Lil for the weekend and what were you wearing on the drive down?' She had very little idea. We both thought it was either March or April and, of course, we couldn't remember what clothes we were wearing on the trip down. That was two or three months ago. Nineteen seventy-six was 516 months ago.

This is what we had going for us:

Firstly, in my statement, I knew what I was doing on the night in question and who I was with earlier in that evening—Chris Fraser, the director of *Summer City*. He had a meeting with me over a meal to discuss the film. I suggested he look at a couple of acting students who I'd seen in plays at NIDA. They ended up being cast for the film. You don't forget the night you got Mel Gibson and Steve Bisley their first jobs in the film industry. This was a huge, unforgettable plus as it allowed me to remember the conversation I had with my false accuser later in the evening when I foolishly weakened to her seduction.

Secondly, in her statement, The Female placed her alleged rape as 'sometime in September 1976' and the Magnetic Island holiday with Rosa in August 1976. My statement had the consensual sex in mid-1976 and the Magnetic Island holiday in October.

We were able to substantiate this with two photographs: one of Rosa in Townsville and the other with The Female and a young man on Magnetic Island. On the back of both photos was stamped '*OCT – 5 –76*', as was customary in those days.

Thirdly, in my statement, in 1986 The Female read in the Cairns newspaper that I was starring in a film called *Dark Age*. She rang the production office, said she was a friend of mine and could they pass on her name and details. I received the message, rang and invited her onto the set. I had no reason not to. I can't recollect ever having a confrontation or argument with her.

The last three weeks of June 2019, to be honest, were a blur. After twenty months, I was finally only twenty-one days from the trial and I could think of nothing else. I read and re-read the police brief. I knew every detail of every statement. And I studied the Randwick house plans, especially the upstairs bedrooms. This is where my acting training came in handy. I absorb scripts, and it's more important for me to know what the film's about, than what the dialogue is. Knowing your script first helps tremendously with remembering the lines, and this training served me well during the trial. I knew my lines.

Chris Murphy would telephone—I love the guy—and he wouldn't say 'hello': he'd go straight on to a very concentrated conversation about evidence, or whatever. He's insanely intelligent so I had to be at the top of my game to keep up. Then he'd snap 'Bye' and hang up. He might ring again five minutes later, or after an hour, five hours, or not at all. On the morning before I had to take the stand, he rang me in bursts, about five times per hour from 5am to 9am. I didn't have time to be nervous. He had me so pumped and prepared I could have played State of Origin.

Chris's right-hand man, Bryan Wrench, will be passed the baton in due course. He's as hungry as Chris to get justice, but he's cooler, not quite as brash. Over the three weeks leading up to the trial, we'd rehearse the probable questions I'd get from my barrister, the astonishing Greg James. Greg is a former Supreme Court judge, and his knowledge of the law is extraordinary; he cites precedents without referring to the law books. His questions were cool, as he was on my side, but the prosecutor's questions—bloody hell!

My lawyer, Bryan, hammered me and scared the pants off me. He said no matter how hard the questions, just answer with the truth, as succinctly as you can. If it's a 'yes' or 'no' answer, answer 'yes' or 'no'. If you answer 'no', followed by three more sentences, that will give the Crown three opportunities to have a go at you. What does a witness do? Answer the questions.

Suddenly it was Friday, 28 June 2019. Suddenly it was real. On the following Monday morning I was going to be standing in a courtroom on trial answering a rape charge. Although I was completely and utterly innocent, it was still daunting. The Female was up first and I knew her dreadful story of my ripping off her clothes and so on would make the headlines. I warned my wife and kids that it was going to be rough. The media writes all the salacious stuff, ignoring any negatives regarding The Female.

It can't help itself. These days, filthy news is good news.

The night before the trial Rosa and I had a kumbaya dinner with our family. My daughters, Zadia and Ebony, my sons Jackson, Riley and Charlie, his wife Maddie, my niece Emma and my surrogate daughter, Jane. Charlie and Maddie had flown in for the trial from Melbourne. Ebony flew in from Alice Springs, leaving our grandkids Jasmine, Phoenix and Leo with her husband, Daniel. Dan is also a computer whiz who ensured he captured every morsel of media coverage. What a family team I had! The strength they gave Rosa and me is beyond description—they were extraordinary. My son, William, couldn't make it as he had commitments in LA with his singing career. I told him to stay there, but he made up for it with hours on the phone.

Day one, 1 July 2019. Driving into the city with Rosa and Ebony was surreal. The conversation was basically that. I was actually going to court on a rape charge. It was fucking weird. We met the family—Zadia, Ebony, Charlie, Maddie, Emma and Jane—for breakfast across the road from my lawyer's office. It was a very sombre affair filled with expectation.

After breakfast I crossed Castlereagh Street to my lawyer's office where I was given the rundown on how the day should pan out. Bryan told me I'd be sitting in the dock for two or three days and the only words I would utter in that time would be 'Not guilty' at the beginning of the proceedings.

At 9.15am, off we went down Elizabeth St to Downing Centre Courts. Past the paparazzi and into the building. We were allocated a court. I went and sat in the dock, feeling like a little boy and completely out of place. Half a dozen chairs in a rectangular box; an emotional torture chamber—I was trapped in a hell hole.

Inside my head I was screaming: 'I don't belong here, this is a massive mistake. Get me out of here, please.' To the people in the gallery I looked calm and composed, as instructed by Chris Murphy and Bryan Wrench. Thankfully, adult John turned up to protect his little boy. 'Man up, you're bigger than this. You're innocent, decent, you have integrity, and you'll not let them beat you—you are strong.' Thank Christ that bloke turned up; he stayed there until the end of the trial.

The jury was selected on the spot, and it didn't take long. About forty people came into court, and the twelve were chosen; seven women and five men of all ages, colours and creeds. They were a fair choice, I thought.

Next the Crown presented its case. Streaming from the prosecutor's mouth was: 'He ripped her bedclothes off, he ripped her underwear off, he ripped her T-shirt off'.

I knew these would be the headlines, and they remained so for the next three days until I had my turn. They were a painful three days for my family, friends, fans and supporters.

After lunch The Female took the stand. She decided to do it by video link. This was fine with me, as I didn't want to be in the same room with her. It was hard to look at her, but I had to. I'm 67 and I'm a bit deaf so it helped to look at her; I didn't want to miss a syllable. I won't comment on how she appeared other than to say, some people look very different from when they were 19. She's now 62.

My observation was that she was very vague and didn't even have a strong grasp of her own written statement. The extraordinary thing was that she continued throughout the rest of the day saying everything took place in 1975 instead of 1976. The Crown kept trying to get her to say 1976 but he couldn't lead her. But she knew something was amiss and in the end she asked to take a break. It was about 3.30pm and the judge decided to quit for the day and continue the next morning.

You'd think she'd go home and reach for her statement and be shocked that she'd got the year wrong all day. It was 1976. Maybe she reached for something else, and here's why...

We resumed at 10am on Tuesday, 2 July. The Crown picked up where it had left off. The prosecutor asked The Female her first question—it was about August 1976. He asked her when it was.

She replied that it was August 1975. August 1975! Wow!

Some say The Female had recreated history and convinced herself her ludicrous story was true. I don't believe that. I think she manufactured the history the week before the trial, and very badly manufactured it, I might add. Here's why: She said she first met me in April 1976 when I answered the door. She immediately recognised me as the actor from *Picnic at Hanging Rock*. She said I was wearing a full-length leather jacket. Why would I wear a full-length leather jacket inside a house in April? She said when I went into her room and 'raped' her I was wearing my full-length leather jacket. She said I raped her while I was fully clothed. She submitted this change to her statement the Wednesday before the trial began. In my mind, involving this leather jacket made me look more of a monster in her eyes and maybe she was hoping the jury would feel the same way. Clearly the fact that it was absurd beyond belief didn't occur to her. She continued with this fiction to the very end.

In her statement, she said that she went on holidays in August with my wife to Magnetic Island and that the alleged rape happened in September. I stated that the consensual sex happened mid-1976 and the Magnetic Island trip happened in September–October. Why would someone who was violently raped go on a holiday shortly afterwards with the rapist's wife? Obviously, because she had not been raped.

Why would she ask her rapist for a job in November on *Summer City* if she'd been recently raped by him? It just doesn't make sense. Why would she see her rapist on and off for the next ten years, culminating with a film called *Dark Age*? Why indeed.

The cross examination of The Female by my barrister, Greg James, was about the film. It was mind boggling and it went something like this:

Greg James: Did you spend time on the set of a film called *Dark Age*?

The Female: No!

Greg James: There's a photo in front of you. Could you tell me who the blonde lady is sitting middle foreground?

The Female: Yes that's me at the wrap party in Cairns. [She'd just lied under oath.]

Greg James: How did you know about the party?

The Female: John Jarratt told me.

Greg James: Did you ring the production office and say you were a friend and get them to give Jarratt your name and number?

The Female: I think so, maybe, yes.

Greg James: Was John Jarratt the star of the film?

The Female: I don't know.

Greg James: What was the name of the film?

The Female: *Razorback*.

Greg James: Wasn't it *Dark Age*?

The Female: No, *Razorback*.

Greg James: Why was John there?

The Female: I don't know, maybe he was visiting.

Greg James: *Razorback* was made in Broken Hill in 1983 and John Jarratt wasn't in it.

The Female: So?

Greg James: Why would you go to a wrap party where your rapist would be?

The Female: I wanted to go, I like a party!

This isn't word for word by any means but it's close—they were the sentiments. This was the person we were dealing with. I can't get over the fact that this woman, despite her ineptitude, wanted to put me in jail for a long time for something she knew I didn't do. I'm continually being asked this and I just don't know. I cannot fathom it. It's hard not to hate her. If I do, it eats me up. I need to send her an exceptional distance from my soul and do my best to delete her so her dark energy never gets in again.

On Tuesday afternoon The Female's cross examination ended. I didn't take my eyes from the screen, I wanted to be looking at her when they turned her off. I wanted that to be the moment I turned her off.

My wife, Rosa, took the stand—she was special with so much poise and dignity. My wife is far and away the most honest person I have met. If your backside looks big in a dress she can't say it doesn't if it does. Her calm and measured responses to being questioned were brave and strong. She's quite shy by nature and it took a ton of guts to talk about her husband having consensual sex while she slept, knowing that the media would be spreading her over every platform that night. She's also Sicilian and The Female messed with her family—my wife is not to be messed with. I'm very proud of her. I'm with an exceptional woman.

Wednesday morning was the cross examining of The Female's witnesses. They were with her after 1976 so their evidence was mainly hearsay and didn't amount to much.

On Wednesday afternoon the police officer went into the stand to be cross-examined by Greg James.

When this whole thing started I was shocked to find out the police investigation would take many months—ten as it turned out. The allegation wasn't thrown out as expected and the police sent their brief to the DDP and they charged me. Because it was an historical allegation of rape they had to take it very seriously and investigate it intensely. They were to leave no stone unturned.

It became increasingly obvious that the police were lucky to have upturned one stone; they did very little for ten months.

A major part of our win was what Chris Murphy, his team and I revealed with our investigation. I'm not a policeman but I read the statements, I saw the anomalies, and I proved her lies and backed it with five-minute Google searches, for instance, when I was in *Season at Sarsaparilla* at the Opera House and when I was working on *Dark Age*, ten years after the alleged rape.

The Female's statement said Judy Davis was sleeping in the next room on the night in question. The Female placed the alleged rape as happening in September. Judy Davis was long gone; we estimate she left in June. Judy stated the reason she left was because she wasn't fond of The Female. Mine and Rosa's statements said Judy Davis was no longer in the house, and Judy's own statement said she had moved out!

The police should have heard alarm bells here. If they'd investigated it, as we did, they'd have come to the conclusion that Judy couldn't have been a witness. It troubles me that Judy was swept up in this mess. This is just one instance where the police fell down on the job they apparently took ten months to do. What were they doing? I feel terribly let down. The punishment for the crime I was facing was five years plus imprisonment. As far as I'm concerned, they put me in danger of being incarcerated through their lack of due diligence and that is outrageous. The number one job is for the police to protect us. But that became the job of Chris Murphy and his diligent team.

The last thing for the day was playing the DVD of me reading my statement at the police station in 2018, where my lawyer said it was OK to express how I felt as long as I kept control. I did just that. I read it compassionately. The last two pages were about how the whole nightmare affected me and my family. It was the first time the jury had heard me speak. I made an impression, a good impression. Finally things were swinging heavily my way.

Finally the press was reporting encouraging views about me. It was a turning point.

Thursday was my turn to take the stand. The Female's statement was unbelievable and ridiculous as far as I was concerned. My statement made sense because it was the truth. I was confident and not at all nervous because I believed in myself and that's all that mattered.

Just before I walked out of the dock and on to the stand I said the Serenity Prayer:

God grant me the serenity
To accept the things I cannot change
Courage to change the things I can
And the wisdom to know the difference.

Suddenly Dad said: 'Sit up straight, look confident, look like you belong'. He said it so powerfully that I answered him out loud. People would have seen my lips move and thought I was nervous. He stayed with me throughout the whole thing, and I had the strength of the toughest bloke I'd ever met.

The Crown didn't lay a glove on me. Mainly there were a lot of 'yes' and 'no' answers. I stayed calm and composed, I wasn't frightened and I never felt challenged. For instance, he asked me if I'd raped The Female and I said no. Did I rip her bedclothes off? 'No.' Did I rip her clothes off? 'No.' Did I mount her fully clothed wearing my full-length leather jacket? Finally I spoke more than 'yes' or 'no'.

'You asked me if I'd raped her and I said no. Now you're asking questions about her fantasy which didn't happen in real life.'

He looked at me for a few seconds and said, 'Did you pin her arms down?'—I replied 'No.' And on it went.

I caught a smile of incredulity from a jury member. The charade stumbled on to its sad conclusion. The members of the jury were bored, they didn't buy it. Bryan said they'd stopped taking notes. A very good sign apparently. I believed it was over.

Bryan said we were miles in front on the scoreboard, but we still needed to tackle hard 'til the end. We didn't want to give them a cheap try.

In the middle of my time on the stand we had a tea break. I had to sit on my own in the dock, and no one was allowed to talk to me. I'd been cross examined about *Summer City*, and Mel Gibson and Steve Bisley were mentioned. As I sat quietly in the dock, I looked towards my friend Steve Bisley sitting quietly in the gallery and we winked at each other. My mobile dinged with a text from Mel Gibson asking me how it was going. I texted back that he'd been mentioned and that I was staring at Steve as I was texting. Bizarre!

Friday was the summations, the closing remarks from the Crown and the defence. The Crown's summation was dry and a bit dull, and again the jury didn't take notes. Greg James' summation, on the other hand, was brilliant. Bryan said it was the best he'd seen. Let's face it, The Female's ridiculous testimony gave him great material to work with. My favourite bit was Greg saying, 'So he came out of the bathroom with his large leather coat belted closed or maybe open and flapping like a bat!'

The jury was given its directions and asked to retire to consider their verdict. It was 12.45pm Friday, 5 June. For the first time, the members were allowed to deliberate. They had fifteen minutes, then they were to break for lunch between 1pm and 2pm. During lunch there was absolutely no deliberation. At 2pm we were all called back into the courtroom and the anxiety on my family's faces broke my heart. That little part of them was saying, 'What if Dad goes to jail?' Zadia was the most pent up. I texted her: 'It's too quick, it's gotta be not guilty'. She smiled nervously back at me.

The judge said: 'We have a unanimous decision'.

The jury foreman stood up: 'Not guilty'. My arms reached for the sky. I turned to my family, all of whom were sobbing. I raced to hug Rosa, but Bryan stole the first one, God bless him. The hug with Rosa was long and deep, and it touched our souls. Then with my beautiful daughters and my wonderful son, who I thought would break my back. We headed for the exit, and Greg James led the charge, a rare thing for him to do. My family fell in love with Greg and wanted to adopt him as their grandfather. He refused on the grounds that he's far too young. It's true, he's a young vibrant man in a mature body.

The paparazzi met us at the entrance and I said a few words which just spilled out: 'No man should have to go through what I've been through. This is my team, this is my wonderful family and this is the love of my life.'

I took my wife under my arm and began to leave as the photographers talked to me while walking backwards with their cameras. I said: 'I don't have to be nice to you people walking backwards any more.'

We strode up Elizabeth Street on Friday afternoon. Bryan said: 'Sing us a song'. I sang 'Freedom' at the top of my lungs as I skipped along the pavement.

I'd like to thank my legal team, especially Byran Wrench, Daniel Murdoch and Dasha, led by the Godfather of Law, Chris Murphy, and my miraculous barrister, Greg James.

I'd like to thank my friends and family for holding me up over the last couple of years, especially our Malibu earth angel—without you all I would have surely fallen.

Most of all I'd like to thank the love of my life, my soul mate, my best friend—yes that's right, my best friend is a woman: my wife, my rock, my Rosa.

I am the victim in this case and yet I've been unemployed since August 2017; my career is on hold. I'm in massive debt and mud has been poured all over my family by the media. My granddaughter was 10 years old when the nightmare began; she's now 12 and has been teased mercilessly at school. You messed with my family and you know who you are.

The perpetrator, in this case The Female who told a lie against me from forty-three years ago, has walked out of the court and it hasn't cost her a cent. She still has a suppression order to protect her identity. From the very beginning I received no such protection. I was hung out to dry, publicly.

This country's present suppression order legislation is illogical and unfair. All I want is a level playing field for all. Is that too much to ask?

When I was 13, I was raped by a large young man. When I was 65, I was accused of rape and nearly two years later, I was exonerated. Does that mean I'm going to shrug, go home and get in the foetal position? No, I'm going to fight because things must change... for the better.

The #MeToo movement needs to continue to out the real predators, the real perverts, the real monsters, with impunity.

I'm going to stand up and play my part.

ALSO BY JOHN JARRATT

The Bastard from the Bush
An Australian Life